THREE WRITERS IN EXILE

THREE WRITERS IN EXILE:

Pound, Eliot & Joyce

by

Doris L. Eder

The Whitston Publishing Company
Troy, New York
1984

CONTENTS

INTRODUCTION

The aim of this study is to discover why three of the most important and influential writers of this century were exiles. Besides asking why Pound, Eliot, and Joyce went into exile, *Three Writers in Exile* seeks answers to the following questions. Why did each writer settle where he did? How did exile make possible or facilitate his work? How did the writer influence his chosen environment and how did his environment influence him? What did each writer retain of his native heritage? What do these authors' works reveal of the state of American, British, and European culture during the first half of this century? Finally, what can we learn about the problem of the alienation of the modern artist by studying the lives and works of Pound, Eliot, and Joyce?

From a host of writers in exile, why choose Pound, Eliot, and Joyce? As exiles these three writers differ from their predecessors. Their exile is more deliberate than that of Henry James, who nevertheless was an example for both Pound and Eliot. James visited Europe and received a European education as a young boy. He grew up with one foot in America and one foot in European culture. In abandoning America at the age of thirty-three, James was giving up only half of his heritage, and then only as Joyce would do later—in order to remember and depict it better from a distance in space and time. The exile of Pound and Eliot was more willed and deliberate than James's. Pound did not see Europe till his teens, Eliot till his twenties. Both went there to do graduate work. Each soon after decided to cut himself off from home and family and a known environment. Joyce's exile, too, was thus deliberate.

The three chosen writers also differ from their successors, the stream of expatriates who headed for Paris after World War I. Since a rigorous definition of exile means permanent removal from home, the American expatriates of the twenties—Cummings, Dos Passos, Fitzgerald, Hemingway, etc.—were not truly exiles. For these writers, Paris was a home away from home. They constituted an American artistic colony in Paris, a coterie of compatriots, speaking English, retaining many of the habits and customs of home. Indeed, one critic says Paris was for these writers "Boystown, U.S.A."[1] They remained unassimilated Yankees. As Gertrude Stein observes, the French are, for the most part, incurious about foreigners and left these Americans to themselves.[2] When the American writers' funds ran out or they grew bored with Paris, they came home. Pound distinguished between this generation and his own. "The new lot of American *emigrés* were anything but the Passionate Pilgrims of James' day or the enquirers of my own. *We* came to find something, to learn, possibly to conserve, but this new lot came in disgust."[3]

In differing degrees, Eliot, Pound, and Joyce settled in and assimilated their adopted environments. They came to stay. In this they may be compared to the writer-emigrants of the thirties, Huxley, Auden, and Isherwood. The turning of the tide into an east-west migration from Europe to the United States coincides with America's taking over, during the thirties, the literary leadership of the English-speaking world, a development Pound did not foresee taking place until the end of the century.

Another reason for choosing to study Pound, Eliot, and Joyce is that the three writers have much else in common besides the fact of being exiles. They knew and influenced each other and might even be said to have formed a kind of mutual admiration society, although Joyce was not given to admiring others. The decisive reason for studying these three is their literary preeminence. Pound, Eliot, and Joyce were all literary pioneers and tastemakers. Pound and Eliot founded new literary movements, and Joyce's technical innovations still occupy his followers. The work of all three great moderns exhibits the characteristic features of modern art in being difficult to the point of obscurity, complex, allusive, experimental in form, and encyclopedic in scope. Though the poetry of Eliot and Pound and some of Joyce's work is pervaded by the romanticism against which they rebelled, their work bears the hallmarks of the new classicism announced by Hulme. The work of all three writers is imbued with the modern attitude to the past—that the past was radically different from the present but eternally haunts it and so is inescapably past-present. *The Waste Land, The Cantos,* and *Ulysses* all make use of the mythic method, juxtaposing past and present for comic, mock-heroic, or tragic effect, always for ironic contrast, and for completeness too, in order, in Eliot's words, to give "a shape and a significance to the immense panorama of futility and anarchy which is contemporary history."[4]

Pound is considered first because he helped launch Eliot's and Joyce's careers, as he did so many others. Eliot was Pound's protégé during his early years in London, and they were literary collaborators for many years. Though Joyce was the eldest of the three, his early publishing difficulties, greater than those encountered by Pound or Eliot, meant that his career got started after Pound's—almost simultaneously with Eliot's—and largely through Pound's help.

Pound's and Eliot's reasons for leaving America were similar. Both artists were alienated intellectuals, repelled, as Henry James had been, by a society in which business was considered the only respectable career for a man. Pound and Eliot early discovered how difficult it would be either to live or to make a living as artists in America. They found America at the turn of the century a cultural desert. They were élitists who disliked democracy's leveling effects and vulgarization of taste and who deplored provincialism and mediocrity. Though they were cosmopolitan, they could not approve the melting pot, and viewed with distaste the hordes of non-Anglo-Saxon immigrants invading the continent and spreading westward. As Midwesterners of English and New England ancestry, both poets felt threatened and doubly displaced. They were exiles in time as well as space. The ideals of the American republic had been tarnished and betrayed in their eyes, first by the election of Andrew Jackson, then by the rampant materialism which succeeded the Civil War. Whereas Pound and Eliot fled a young giant of a civilization, flexing its muscles in its prime, Joyce was in flight from moribund Ireland. Joyce's work, from first to last, holds a mirror up to the provincialism, stagnation, and death-in-life of Dublin during the first decade of the century.

Europe drew Pound, Eliot, and Joyce because it was the treasurehouse of culture. With its age-old cities, its great monuments, museums, and libraries, it offered them the artistic milieu and resources they craved and lacked in their homelands. Joyce may not have experienced a cultural deprivation and hunger as great as Pound's or Eliot's, but he felt himself on the margins of the western cultural imperium. All three writers were Francophiles; Paris was for Eliot and Joyce their first port-of-call. Pound viewed the center of western civilization as the "double city" of London-Paris. For all three, Europe provided a way of life more artistic, enticing, and exciting than any they could find or make for themselves at home. To be in the company of fellow artists was another strong inducement for going abroad. James noted that in Hawthorne's time the literary profession was honored in America, but that there were so few serious writers on such a large continent that they were isolated. James further observed, "The best things come . . . from . . . talents that are members of a group; every man works better when he has companions working in the same line, yielding the stimulus of suggestion, comparison, consultation. . . . The solitary worker loses the profit of example and discussion; he is apt to make awkward experiments."[5]   During the early years of the century, when Pound and Eliot were embarking on their careers, writers remained isolated, but the profession of writing was no longer esteemed in America. Pound, in particular, a born teacher and impresario, needed collaborators. His collaboration with Eliot was only one of many that proved fruitful and influential; had they attempted it in the United States, it probably would have encountered greater obstacles and been stillborn. Pound experienced great difficulty publishing his early poems in his native land. Not until Pound became *Poetry's* London correspondent, tirelessly promoting from abroad the best new work, did the American poetic renaissance get underway. Before World War I, a spate of little magazine and experimental publishing houses began to flourish, however briefly, in both Europe and America. Pound was largely responsible for creating this literary market for modern poetry, fiction, and criticism. His own most awkward and dangerous experiments were made later, in isolation, in Rapallo. Of the three writers, Joyce was the one most clearly driven into exile in order to *write*. Joyce's scrupulous naturalism with its fidelity to detail and habit of naming names, together with his satiric vein, meant that he early ran afoul of Dublin publishers. He soon realized he would never be able to publish his major works in Ireland. Experience was to prove him correct. Like so many Irishmen, in order to write he had to go abroad—not that Europe would furnish his subject matter (as it did, to some extent, Pound's and Eliot's), but so that, from Trieste, Zurich, and Parish he could put Dublin forever on the world's literary map.

How each writer traveled and where he chose to settle is revealing of the character and aims of each, although all three were cosmopolitan city-dwellers. In 1908 Pound headed first for Venice; he had first seen Venice ten years earlier and it had been love at first sight. Northern Italy remained Pound's terrestrial paradise, the place he most enjoyed living in, although it was difficult to make a living there. After publishing his first volume of poems in Venice at his own expense, Pound traveled to London. He was inevitably drawn to one of the twin capitals of western civilization, to Yeats, whom he considered the greatest living poet, and to the company of his own kind. The twelve years Pound spent in London were his most productive, as both poet and promoter of the arts, although everywhere he went he established a beachhead for modern art, whether poetry, fiction, sculpture, or music. In 1920 the dead, disillusioned, and disillusioning atmosphere of postwar London and Pound's own loss of publishing outlets drove him to Paris. Paris was, of course, *the* place for an artist to be after the war. On the one hand, Pound welcomed the opportunity to play mandarin again to a circle of international artists; on the other, he hoped to settle down to his own work on *The Cantos,* begun five years before and projected to keep him occupied for another forty. But after only four years there, the City of Light seemed to the restless poet effete, played out. He returned to Italy, this time to the small seaside town of Rapallo, discovered in *villeggiatura* on the Riviera.

Pound flourished at the center of civilization. When he felt civilization, seemingly exhausted in London and Paris, had failed him, he proposed to set up his own on the shores of the Mediterranean. He anticipated for Italy a new fascist *Rinascimento,* a recrudescence of *virtú.* Rapallo finally gave him the solitude he needed to write the bulk of *The Cantos,* though he continued to be an impresario of poetry and music and a one-man university to disciples who would visit him to be indoctrinated either in poetry or economics. Pound spent twenty-one years in Rapallo. His relative isolation there exerted a baneful influence on him. Self-opinionation and eccentricity degenerated into fanaticism and megalomania, for want of intercourse with intellectual equals and exposure to other views than his own. Pound's social, economic, political, and cultural ideas had always been simplistic; now they became absurd and dangerous *idées fixes.* For his broadcasts over Rome Radio in which he praised the fascists and denounced the Allies, Pound was arrested as a traitor in May 1945 and in November flown to the United States.

Declared insane and unfit to stand trial for treason, he spent the next thirteen years of his life confined in a lunatic asylum, an exile within his own country, alienated in the most literal sense. On release, Pound returned to Italy.

Pound was a born traveler, a tourist. He loved visiting new places, meeting new people, learning new languages, soaking up a new ambience—all were potent means of "making it new." Not so Eliot. To Eliot Pound appeared a squatter who resisted settling into any environment, whereas Eliot felt a profound need to put down roots. Eliot's first love had been Paris, not London, and he had seriously considered settling in Paris and writing in French. This was not to be. In August 1914, when war broke out, Eliot was studying in Germany. He hastened to England, where he had already enrolled for a course of graduate study in philosophy at Oxford. It was Pound who urged his friend to turn to a literary career, who helped publish his first poems, who got him a job, and who encouraged his marriage to an Englishwoman. (Pound was himself married to an Englishwoman.) Pound did all this because he recognized Eliot's genius and saw that London was the best medium for Eliot's sober, persistent, essentially imperialistic literary talent. Eliot himself came to realize that there was no better place for him to put down roots than the country of his ancestors. Rarely has anyone so thoroughly repatriated himself. England combined the charm of familiarity with that of difference, while France came to seem too alien and too stimulating. England further offered the enormous advantage of allowing Eliot to cleave to the mother tongue and, as a spokesman for British culture, of enabling him to mediate, as James had, between the New and Old Worlds.

Joyce, like Pound, felt a *Drang nach Suden,* preferring Southern to Northern Europe. Like Pound he had the tourist mentality, but he was much less observant of his surroundings and less particular in his choice of abode. Joyce's hegira was outwardly more casual, even less planned than Pound's rather hectic odyssey. When Joyce left Ireland in 1904, he did not know where he would go but left his fate in the hands of Berlitz. Berlitz first sent him to Pola, the "naval Siberia" of the Adriatic, as Joyce called it. He was then transferred to Trieste, a city he came, over a decade, to like. War drove him to Zurich, a refuge for exiles from all over Europe and a hotbed of experimentalism in the arts, a suitable background for the gestation of *Ulysses.* It was Pound who persuaded Joyce to remove from

Trieste (to which he had returned when the war ended) to Paris, so that he too might be at the artistic hub of the universe. Thus Joyce returned to the scene of his first sojourn in Europe; Paris had been for him, as for Eliot, his original refuge from home in 1902. Joyce remained in Paris for nineteen years, until war once again drove him to Zurich, where he died.

Joyce was a globetrotter like Pound but, whereas Pound's surroundings mattered to him, Joyce's really did not, so long as he could write. Indeed, due to poor eyesight, Joyce perceived his surroundings only with difficulty. Wherever he went was for Joyce merely a dim background against which to project and record his vivid memories of Ireland in his youth. Outwardly as rootless as Pound, Joyce was not inwardly so. His life and art were transfixed, rooted in the Dublin he had known as a young man, which was the subject of all his work. Joyce's exile, has, like Pound's, the appearance of flight, but that flight is undertaken for the sake of imaginative release—and, above all, return. So that it may be said of Joyce, as of Eliot, that his end was his beginning and his beginning, his end.

Inquiring into the influence each writer exerted on his environment and vice versa, one must distinguish between the physical and literary environments. The influence of all three writers on the patria of letters has been a great and continuing one. The influence of their environments on them is not as palpable as one might expect. Because Eliot took root in his adopted environment as neither Pound nor Joyce did, the influence Eliot exerted on that environment, and its influence on him, were strongest. Eliot sought and found in England an organic society which satisfied his hunger for tradition and order; society, politics, and religion were more closeknit and institutionalized in England than in the United States. Eliot's criticism tends to be socio-political and religious as well as literary. So profound was Eliot's influence that he became virtually London's literary dictator from the twenties through the forties. England constituted for him a bridgehead between Europe and America. Eliot's influence, like Pound's, spanned the Atlantic, and, if we consider his influence on the New Criticism, may be considered to have lasted into the fifties and sixties.

Though Eliot and Pound share a nostalgia for world culture, Eliot paradoxically identifies universality with localism.[6] Yet Eliot himself seems an exception to his own rule. His poetry is universal, but there is little in it that is specifically local. When we look at his poems for physical evidence of his adopted country, we find little. Such images as there are of city, village, church, or stately home are universalized, made symbolic. So are the even fewer images of his native land. Eliot's criticism and drama, however, do bear an increasingly English stamp.

Pound's influence on his successive environments was vital, but Pound did not stay put. Whatever town he lived in could not help but be aware of his lively presence, for Pound spent as much time and energy promoting art as practicing it. Thus, even in Rapallo, where he was no longer center of a literary coterie, as he had been in London and Paris, Pound became a musical impresario, sponsoring a series of concerts of fine but rarely performed works. Because he was entrepreneur, practitioner, teacher, and factotum in many different arts, Pound's influence was widespread. In aspiring to be a modern Renaissance man, Pound was active not only in literature, but in art, music, and sculpture, politics, and economics. As a literary promoter alone, he helped launch the careers of Aiken, Aldington, Bunting, Frost, H. D., Hulme, Wyndham Lewis, Marianne Moore, William Carlos Williams, and Zukofsky, as well as those of Eliot and Joyce. As Eliot observed, Pound's most important contribution to the arts was that he made modern poetry possible on both sides of the Atlantic. Because Pound was aggressive, however, he aroused hostility and resistance wherever he went, which eventually propelled him elsewhere.

Pound's poetry shows he was sensually alive to his surroundings as neither Eliot nor Joyce was. (Yet he could summon a self-preserving imperviousness—witness his thirteen years in St. Elizabeth's, where what saved him was apparent obliviousness of his surroundings.) Examining Pound's work, one finds vivid images of the many places he lived in or visited—of Venice, Sirmione, Rapallo, Pisa, Provence, Paris and London.

Though Joyce's influence on the novel has been enormous and is still felt today, the influence on him of his various places of exile was minimal. It is as though Dublin had been branded so deeply on his mind as to preclude his being influenced by any other environment. Joyce's Dublin-obsessed fiction could have been written anywhere, the only indication of where it was written being the author's concise notification of the city in which he began and ended each book. Joyce's deteriorating eyesight, steadily worsening as he moved from Trieste to Zurich to

Paris, made it possible for him to see the outside world only through a glass darkly. So Joyce developed a style more aural than visual, less "the reflection of the glowing sensible world through the prism of a language manycoloured and richly storied than . . . the contemplation of an inner world of individual emotions mirrored perfectly in a lucid supple periodic prose."[7]

The work of all three artists, despite its cosmopolitanism, does bear the mark of their origins. This is more obviously true of Joyce than of Pound or Eliot. Neither Pound's nor Eliot's work is local as Joyce's is. Though exile was the means by which Joyce accomplished his work and is itself one of his abiding themes, Dublin is the subject of his entire *oeuvre.* The single-mindedness with which Joyce recalled and recorded his native heritage is unique. The density of the Irish social environment contrasts strikingly with the thinness of Eliot's and Pound's American ambience, explaining why Dublin was not something Joyce could simply slough off, but had internalized and had to carry around with him for the rest of his life. Though all three writers were internationalists who made great Europeans of themselves, Pound's essential Americanness is no less patent than Joyce's quintessential Irishness. Pound remained an American to the last. He might have saved himself years of anguish and imprisonment by abandoning his nationality, but he never considered himself anything but an American. Eliot repatriated himself and we may view him, like James, as an oddly dual, transatlantic figure, but Eliot himself insists the emotional springs of his poetry are American, and the work of both Eliot and James evinces an unmistakably New England moral conscience.

Pound and Eliot emphasized and seem to have prided themselves on their Anglo-Saxon origins. Indeed, both poets are nineteenth century men in the importance they attach to the idea of race. They regarded themselves as authentic Americans. Non-WASP immigrants were not authentic Americans, and by coming to the United States they had ceased to be authentic anything else. Pound and Eliot approved of diversity of races, preservation of ethnic customs, and local color when they met with these in Europe. Yet the distinctive ethnic groups of America's immigrant neighborhoods filled them with disdain and dismay. Perhaps they regarded the Jews and Italians in America as corrupt, debased, or culturally debilitated by the melting pot of United States society. Perhaps they saw these "hyphenates" as destined to merge into an indistinguishable American amalgam, without contributing any cultural flavor of their own. The American melting pot, instead of promoting heterogeneity or the diversity-within-unity of a country like Britain or Italy, produced uniformity and conformity.

Exile is thought to exact a heavy toll of a writer. An exile loses his roots; thus an exiled writer's hold on his subject matter, which is usually what he knows best, is undermined. In an essay in which he says a writer's subject matter is racial and comprises the experience of his first twenty-one years, Eliot uses the concept of race to include cultural as well as ethnic heritage.[8] Eliot thus viewed his own youth as rooted in a particular race, family, and locality. He seems to have been influenced by the ideas expressed in Van Wyck Brooks's *The Wine of the Puritans,* which he reviewed for the *Harvard Advocate.* Van Wyck Brooks or his persona argues that the greatest art springs from materials existing in the artist "by instinct and which constitute racial fibre, the accretion of countless generations of ancestors, trained to one deep, local, indigenous attitude toward life."[9] The artist's soul is the product of his particular race, generation, and locality. Neither Pound's nor Eliot's roots in America, however, were as deeply embedded as Joyce's roots in Ireland. Pound resolved to deliver himself from the great grey expanse of the Middle West, reversing the westward migration of his forebears across the American continent by his own eastward migration across Europe. Eliot migrated to England to regraft himself on the original Elyot stock.

A study of exile should investigate why some artists stay put and others go abroad. The twentieth century has engendered an enormous number of writers in exile: James, Conrad, Stephen Crane, Gertrude Stein, Ford Madox Ford, Eliot, Pound, Miller, Lawrence, Beckett, Nabokov, Huxley, Auden, and Isherwood are some of the writers who went into permanent exile. Many more, including a goodly number of Americans, traveled extensively abroad—Edith Wharton, Fitzgerald, Hemingway, Aiken, Cummings, and Dos Passos, among others. The number of eminent writers who stayed put may come to seem small by comparison: Faulkner, Frost (after a sojourn in England, where he first became known), Stevens, Williams, Marianne Moore, and some local colorists.

In the great stay-put-or-leave controversy between in-

digenous and expatriate American artists, in which William Carlos
Williams and Ezra Pound were opposing spokesmen, Pound per-
versely argued that it was Williams' foreign blood which enabled
him to stay in America by inoculating him against the native
virus which compelled Pound and Eliot to leave. This virus
Pound identified with the thin blood and cerebralism of New
England.[10] Thus there is the paradox that, on their own ad-
mission, Williams' mixed blood impelled him to cling to America, while Pound's WASP ancestry compelled him to leave.
Williams' position was that of a second generation American
immigrant: he was a foreigner longing to belong. One reason
Pound and Eliot felt they did not belong was because their race
and class were being superseded by the flood of non-Anglo-
Saxon immigrants to the United States.

What is there to be said for Williams' localism against
Pound's and Eliot's internationalism? Williams insists the local,
what is here and now, *is* the universal. He identifies integrity of
imagination with its integration with "genius of place." The
artist's material must be what he has felt and known most directly and sustainedly. Further, Williams adopts Kandinsky's artistic
principles in *Concerning the Spiritual in Art.* According to Kandinsky, the artist must express himself, his epoch (which includes
his place as well as his time), and finally, his art must be part of
the art of all ages and places, that is, it must partake of universality. According to Williams, however, the more purely artistic,
universal, and eternal art is, the less it will express the artist's personality or address his contemporaries and fellow citizens.
Williams used his argument to disparage the universal, impersonal, sometimes timeless and placeless art of Eliot and Pound.
(To the timeless and placeless art of Joyce in *Finnegans Wake*
Williams raised no objection, presumably because Joyce had already thoroughly expressed his locality in his early works.)[11]

In theory Eliot sometimes agrees with Williams, as when he
argues that an artist must be local before he can be universal. In
practice, however, Eliot is not local. Neither is Pound. And
there are many other artists who do not bear out Williams' point
of view. The art of James, Conrad, Lawrence, Fitzgerald, Hemingway, Nabokov, Beckett, Huxley, and Auden, among others,
is not confined to these writers' native localities. A strenuous
localist might argue that the best work of some of these writers
deals with their native places. On the other hand, one may cite
such mavericks as Conrad and Stevens. Conrad never wrote

about his native country. Stevens stayed put in Hartford as determinedly as Williams in Rutherford, yet Stevens' poetry is wholly independent and reveals nothing of his region. It could as well have been written in Paris as Connecticut.

Williams' theory contains an essential truth about the value of lived experience, but shows that common sense pushed to an extreme becomes absurd. We must remember that it was conceived, as most artistic theories are, to explain and vindicate his own life's work. James's insistence that the artist be someone on whom nothing is lost is more important than fidelity to one's original or any single environment. If an artist is observant, his material may be drawn from any milieu in which he finds himself. Beyond observation, if his imagination is sufficiently powerful, he may evoke experiences he has never in fact experienced. The artist's first allegiance is to the country inside his own head. Thus, Gertrude Stein observes in *Paris France*: "everyone who writes is interested in living inside themselves in order to tell what is inside themselves. That is why writers have to have two countries, the one where they belong and the one in which they live really. The second one is romantic, it is separate from themselves, it is not real but it is really there."[12] Still, one acknowledges that the environment in which an artist spent his formative years is likely to have molded and to dominate his imagination in some way. Thus Eliot declares the experiences of his first twenty-one years are the artist's subject. No doubt it was so with Eliot, but his art shows precious little of the locality in which he grew up. The influences of his first twenty-one years are negative, spectral presences, but then his art is one of omission, obliquity, and ellipsis.

Williams' rooting of art in its immediate environment reminds one of Pound's cleaving to concrete particulars. The common source of both poets' theories was Imagism. Pound's poetic theory may be more flexible and accommodating than Williams'; nevertheless, some of Williams' criticisms of Pound are pointed and cogent. Though Pound never abandons the concrete, in his poetry the present yields to the past and the immediate to the literary too often. Thus, much of Pound's poetry has a precious, archaic quality. Eliot's poetry is as literary and equally in thrall to the past, yet, in comparison with Pound's, it appears both more modern and more enduring. It seems to owe less to others and more to his own sensibility. Eliot's images, whether of the damp souls of housemaids sprouting in areaways or of ragged claws scuttling across the oceanbed, are as suggestive as they are concrete and are set against the immense background of time-space. They conform to Pound's definition of the image by presenting an emotional and intellectual complex in an instant of time in such a way as to give a feeling of liberation from temporal and spatial limits.[13]   One would argue against Williams that, though Eliot's poetry achieves universality without being local, it speaks to us no less persuasively for that.

Williams asserted that when Pound left America for Europe he took with him only enough raw material for poetry to last him two years.[14]   Williams presumably meant by this that Pound's poetic baggage comprised a limited store of impressions garnered from his native environment.   Williams well knew Pound's lively and sensuous temperament; he must also have known that Pound did not inhabit Wyncote or America but a world of books, a scholar's world.   Pound was haunted by the beauty of the past and in Europe sought the same.   Van Wyck Brooks opines: "I think it would be well for our artists to discover how soon the training they gain abroad and the vitalizing effects of this fellowship with all that beauty in the past has given to these older civilizations, cease to be a preparation for their own self-expression and becomes [*sic*] an overmastering impulse leading them hither and thither, and merging them intermittently in the artistic consciousness of Spain and Italy and France, unable to carry them below the technique of any. They cannot graft themselves upon the racial tradition that has produced any of the great masters, and they find themselves indeed in sympathy with many races but curiously outside all."[15]   This was written at the turn of the century when there was little native American tradition in literature or painting and American artists had to go abroad in search of tradition or stay at home and forget it.   Van Wyck Brooks defines a dilettante as "an artist without a country."[16]   Pound was that, as neither Joyce nor Eliot was.   Van Wyck Brooks's previous observations also seem to apply to Pound.   Disciple of so many great masters and master of so many different techniques, is he himself a great master?   Has not the cultivation of technique perhaps estranged him from himself, cutting off self-expression at the root?   Pound's poetry is frequently ventriloquial; one is often hard put to it to locate the self it expresses.

Did exile impoverish the art of these three writers, making it thin and etiolated?   The loss of roots they had always felt to be precarious was less damaging to Eliot and Pound than it might have been if their subject matter had been less bookish. Since the late nineteenth century, since the practice of art as a religion, literature has tended to be self-reflexive, becoming its own place, a city of words, as Tony Tanner calls it. This has made it easier for writers to be nomadic; when one's subject matter is literature itself, it becomes portable. Though Joyce was a Flaubertian artist *par excellence,* his subject matter was not books, but life as he knew it in Dublin. His exile was motivated wholly by the desire for freedom of expression. Joyce carried his subject matter with him for the rest of his life, stored like the water in a camel's hump. Henry James went into exile in search of his actual subject matter. For him the novel was necessarily about customs, manners, usages; in America these were insufficient or insufficiently distinctive for his taste. He spent a lifetime assaying American and English culture. Strictly speaking, Pound and Eliot need not have gone abroad for their material, since this was largely to be found in books and in the past. Europe was, however, precisely on this account the ideal place of exile for them, but the literariness and pastness of Pound's and Eliot's work help explain why Europe of the twentieth century figures in it less than one would expect. There is more in Pound than in Eliot: the *Pisan Cantos,* for example, stand out from all the rest for their immediacy, their quality of lived experience.

After several years of exile Joyce complained that Ireland was becoming a mist in his brain. The damage separation from his subject matter might have done Joyce's work was mitigated by his surrounding himself with family. Nora in particular symbolized Erin for Joyce. He also kept up an assiduous correspondence with family and friends in Dublin and avidly absorbed news of Ireland. Poetry travels better than the novel. Yet there does seem to be a point at which constant uprooting of the poet damages poetry as well. It is fashionable to set a higher value on Eliot's early than on his late poetry, but it is clear this work as a whole profited from his settling in England. Even if England contributes little more local color to Eliot's work than America, it was good for a poet with a demonic view of art to lead a settled, ordered, rooted life. One feels sure Pound would have benefited from a more settled existence.

Warner Berthoff concludes that the question of whether to remain in the United States and devote oneself to producing an indigenous art, or whether to avail oneself of a typically

American freedom in order to leave and create a cosmopolitan art elsewhere is really a red herring. The important thing, whether one stays or leaves, is learning to write.[17] Such a conclusion would not have satisfied Williams, for he believed America would breed a unique consciousness and particular techniques to express it. The empirical evidence shows that some artists found it easier to learn to write and certainly to publish abroad. Of these, some remained abroad (Pound and Eliot) and some returned home (most of the twenties expatriates). Though much fiction and poetry about America was written from the vantage point of Europe, some authors learned to write and to make a reputation at home. The case of Wallace Stevens suggests it makes little difference where a man writes, but he is a special case, an example of the triumph of an intelligence over a soil that Williams himself acknowledged to be recalcitrant.

Despite the loss of roots, exile offers distinct advantages. It enables one to see and to experience much that is new and different from what one is accustomed to. Exposure to other lands and languages, climates and customs is a tonic. It is exhilarating and sharpens one's pleasure in life; it prevents provincialism, complacency, and boredom. In assessing the difference between the foreign and the familiar, one acquires a dual viewpoint which is immensely valuable. Such a dual viewpoint entails and reinforces that simultaneous sense of detachment and involvement which is an essential feature of the writer's attitude to his subject matter, whether that subject is native or alien. And the dual point of view can lead to a sense of proportion, to a feeling for what is important, enduring, and valuable, and what is not. Thus Pound made it his life's work to discover what was permanent, what recurrent, and what merely transitory in poetry.

Nothing could be more appropriate to the production of such cosmopolitan work than the travel and exile which gave Pound, Eliot, and Joyce knowledge of many different languages, cultures, and societies. Terry Eagleton, in his book *Exiles and Emigrés,* tries to account for the fact that twentieth century English literature has been dominated by a Pole (Conrad), three Americans (James, Eliot and Pound), two Irishmen (Yeats and Joyce), and only one native born Englishman (Lawrence). (Lawrence, though English, was an outsider, a "spy" from the lower classes.)[18] Eagleton comes to the conclusion that these outsiders, because they brought with them larger frames of reference, were able to achieve a more total view of English society than any that could be achieved by an insider. The total point of view is not a local point of view—that is precisely the point. Totality of vision is, however, most valuable, it is what we most need today, and is perhaps the outstanding achievement of the art of Eliot, Pound, and Joyce.

What picture of the state of American, British, and European culture of their time does Pound's, Eliot's, and Joyce's work present us with? Pound and Joyce both experienced Europe in the halcyon days before World War I. Eliot did so only briefly. He was on the spot in Germany in 1914 to witness the spectacle of Europe committing suicide. The most important period of each writer's career lay between two world wars. All three writers present vividly detailed impressions of modern urban industrial society on the point of breakdown. Fragmented form reflects a world in fragments, all coherence gone; Europe, its old center, cannot hold. And yet to say this is to paint too dismal a picture, for these three writers are grand conservators. They have catalogued the contents of the museum of western culture before it is utterly sacked and ruined. How impoverished modern literature would be without Joyce's detailed Flemish portraits of Dublin and Dubliners, without the idyllic pastorals and exquisite Chinese scenes in Pound's *Personae* and *Cantos,* or without the calm, mystic beauty and peace of Eliot's *Four Quartets,* the reverse of the frenetic motion grounded and mired in despair in *The Waste Land.*

As *avant-gardistes,* Pound, Eliot, and Joyce exhibit characteristic features of artistic alienation. Pound and Eliot conform to a typical avant garde pattern in being artistically radical but politically reactionary.[19] Their rightwing politics are the result of these artists' hostility to democratic liberalism, of their desire for a *rappel à l'ordre,* and also perhaps of their nostalgia for a past in which the artist held a secure and respected position in society. It is interesting that in the early Middle Ages the poet was considered the opposite or antitype of the exile. Enthroned in the bosom of society, at the feet of the king, the poet or maker exercised an art reminiscent of God's Creation. The exile, on the other hand, was someone *persona non grata* who was cast out, amputated from the community. Exile was once considered a more severe punishment than death and was reserved for the highest crimes—murder and treason. But the figure of the artist later fused with that of the exile when the bard had to travel from place to place to recite his works before different communities.[20] Still the poet was an honored and valued member of the community. With the breakdown of the system of artistic patronage and the rise of a mass market for print, writers were driven into enclaves within an indifferent or hostile society. Since the romantic age, the artist has been socially, economically, and politically estranged from society. Joyce in his youth was a socialist because he believed only a socialist state would subsidize the artist in devoting his life to juggling words on a page.

The principal sources of alienation are somewhat different in Joyce, Eliot, and Pound. Joyce's alienation is explicitly detailed in *Dubliners* and *A Portrait of the Artist as a Young Man.* Joyce rejected his home, family, society, nation, and religion. In a letter to Nora Barnacle, written when he was twenty-one, Joyce declares: "My mind rejects the whole present social order and Christianity—home, the recognized virtues, classes of life, and religious doctrines. . . . I cannot enter the social order except as a vagabond."[21] Socially Joyce was declassed, a displaced person; his father was a gentleman's only son, but was so feckless and improvident that his own numerous children grew up in dire poverty. As the eldest, James had at an early age to make the difficult adjustment from relative prosperity to hunger and misery. Joyce felt isolated even within the family circle, maintaining that only one of his numerous brothers and sisters understood him, his brother Stanislaus. Like Eliot, Joyce sought a mate outside his class, and as with Eliot, this "misalliance" set the seal on his exile, particularly as he did not intend to marry Nora Barnacle. Joyce's alienation is thus as total as can be imagined, embracing family, society, culture, nation, sex, and religion.

Eliot, like Joyce, came of a large family and had only one brother to whom he was close. Unlike Joyce, Eliot was the youngest child; the large gap in age between him and his elder sisters probably enhanced his sense of loneliness and difference. Eliot's alienation is neither as extreme nor as all-encompassing as Joyce's. He found America's socio-political, aesthetic, and religious climate uncongenial, not intolerable, as Joyce found Ireland's. Compared with Joyce and Pound, Eliot was an accommodationist who needed and knew how to find his place in society. Eliot's alienation, however, went beyond the temporal or geographical; it was felt most deeply as a religious lack. The least in love with life of these three writers, Eliot needed an allegiance to the supernatural. He made his peace with society, though a split between man and artist, bourgeois and poet is observable throughout his career.

Pound was an only child whose relationship with his parents was mutually affectionate and admiring. No one has yet suggested the sources of his alienation lay in his early family life. Pound's revulsion was, like Eliot's, against a time and place inimical to art, but it was much more violent. The alienation Pound felt was aesthetic and economic. His interest in money, encouraged by his father's position as Assayer at the Mint, manifested itself very early. Though an aesthete, Pound was also a man of action and found it difficult to divorce poetry from politics on that account. The role his publishing difficulties played in driving him further and further into his obsessive and eccentric study of economics cannot be overestimated. Pound's restlessness, energy, volatility, and arrogance contrast strongly with Eliot's quietness, modesty, patience, and perseverance. Pound became his own worst enemy, exhibiting and arousing overt hostility in successive environments and destroying carefully cultivated literary outlets through an outspoken impatience with stupidity. Charles Norman convincingly suggests that Pound suffered self-alienation, that his extreme nomadic restlessness in middle age was a running away from himself.[22] The actions which led to Pound's incarceration in St. Elizabeth's show how extreme his estrangement from reality was. Pound's alienation was more virulent and much less controlled than Joyce's or Eliot's.

In conclusion, Pound, Eliot, and Joyce exemplify three different kinds of exile. Eliot uprooted himself from America in order to transplant himself elsewhere. In England he found a society and mental climate congenial to his temperament and settled there. Being a writer compelled Joyce to leave his homeland. Though his love-hate relationship with Ireland was even more intense than Pound's ambivalence toward America, Joyce remained faithful to Ireland in spirit. Abroad, he made it his life's work to create the uncreated conscience of his race and to recreate Dublin down to the last detail. Asked when he would return to Dublin, Joyce answered, "Have I ever left it?"[23] Pound offers the most complete example of alienation and exile of the three. Alienated from America, he never found a home elsewhere, though Italy came closest. Unlike Eliot, Pound felt no need to belong to any land, people, class, or faith. His family life was, in some respects, more irregular than Joyce's and less closeknit. There are radical discontinuities in Pound's life and work. His psychology is insufficiently understood. One is tempted to attribute his capriciousness and lack of capacity for sustained attention or thought to Pound's lack of stable environment. Conversely, his shunning a stable environment is probably the result of an essentially flighty personality. The increasing eccentricity which finally landed him in a madhouse is largely due to the mental isolation in which Pound lived from his forties onward. One of his poems expresses Pound's desire to live "Out, and alone, among some / Alien people!"[24] In doing so all his life, Pound became completely deracinated, with unhappy effects on his work. Thus we see, beyond certain similarities in their work, striking contrasts in the lives of these three writers in exile. These should enable us better to understand them and the general problem of the alienation of the modern artist.

Finally, a brief explanation and declaration of thanks are in order. I undertook this study because, as an exile myself, I am particularly interested in this fascinating subject. What incites one to abandon the known for the unknown, what are the effects of transplantation, and what the ultimate advantages and disadvantages of exile? In seeking answers to the questions raised at the beginning about each of these writers, different problems were encountered. In Pound's case, there are several biographies and certain of his letters expatiate in lively fashion on the subject of his exile. What is lacking is a judicious and thorough psychological study of the poet.

Eliot remains, as he intended, something of an enigma. His will stipulated that no biography of him be written. Valerie Eliot, however, is now looking for a biographer as a result of several inaccurate or self-serving pseudo-biographies written by people who knew Eliot only slightly. The deepest causes of Eliot's alienation and his most personal reasons for leaving the United States are not yet known; I suspect they were familial. By contrast, the reasons for Joyce's exile and its effects upon him are clear. Exile is one of his obsessive subjects and he himself exhaustively documents the reasons for his alienation from Ireland. Further evidence is provided by Ellmann's monumental biography.

The Pound or Eliot scholar faces problems of access to restricted material. The archives of the Beinecke Library at Yale contain a wealth of material on Pound, including the Schloss Brunnenberg collection purchased from Pound's daughter, Princess Mary de Rachewiltz. These archives are available to scholars for research. After Pound was officially declared insane, his literary property rights were entrusted to his wife, Dorothy. In 1974, after the deaths of Pound and his wife, these rights were transferred to the three-man Ezra Pound Literary Property Trust. James Laughlin of New Directions continues to act as agent for the Trust, as he did for Dorothy Pound. The materials in the Yale archives have now been processed and a register prepared by the library staff.

Harvard and Princeton both have much restricted or closed Eliot material, some of which cannot be seen until the year 2000. An official biography of Eliot awaits the publication of Valerie Eliot's four volume edition of her late husband's letters. Eliot destroyed many of his letters, which were, in any case, habitually very reticent. Judging from the unpublished letters I have read, I do not think examination of further Eliot correspondence would help solve the remaining riddles of his exile. It may be these will forever remain a mystery; this was certainly Eliot's intention.

Three Writers in Exile occupied me during two years of writing and research. Fellowships from the University of Rochester enabled me to visit and study Pound, Eliot, and Joyce archives at Yale, Harvard, Princeton, the Humanities Research Center of the University of Texas at Austin, the University of Pennsylvania, the State University of New York at Buffalo, and Cornell. I wish to express thanks to Donald Gallup for his bibliographical help and for guiding me to the material most likely to assist my study; to James Laughlin for granting me, on behalf of the Ezra Pound Literary Property Trust, permission to quote from unpublished Pound Letters; to Valerie Eliot for kindly answering my questions and enabling me to examine unpublished and restricted Eliot correspondence, and to David Farmer of the Humanities Research Center of the University of Texas at Austin. Most of all I thank husband and friends for help and moral support during my quest.

NOTES

[1] Warner Berthoff, *The Ferment of Realism: American Literature, 1884-1919* (New York: Free Press, 1965), p. 298.

[2] *Paris France* (New York: Charles Scribner's Sons, 1940), p. 17.

[3] *Make It New: Essays by Ezra Pound* (New Haven: Yale University Press, 1935), p. 14.

[4] "*Ulysses,* Order and Myth" in Seon Givens, ed., *James Joyce: Two Decades of Criticism* (New York: Vanguard Press, 1948), p. 201.

[5] *Hawthorne* (New York: Doubleday & Company, n.d.), pp. 33-34.

[6] "American Literature and the American Language," in Allen Tate, ed., *The Sewanee Review,* Eliot Memorial Issue, 74 (January-March 1966), 14.

[7] James Joyce, *A Portrait of the Artist as a Young Man* (New York: The Viking Press, 1956), p. 166.

[8] "Turgenev," *The Egoist,* 4 (December 1917), 167.

[9] *The Wine of the Puritans* (New York: M. Kennerley, 1909), p. 121.

[10] Letters nos. 137 & 170 to William Carlos Williams, *Selected Letters of Ezra Pound, 1907-41,* ed. D. D. Paige (New York: New Directions, 1971), pp. 124 and 158.

[11] *Selected Essays of William Carlos Williams* (New York: Random House, 1954), pp. 75-79.

[12] P. 2. In context, Stein seems to identify the first country as America, the second as France. The passage also implies that the first country is mental, the second, geographical. The statement is so ambiguous and suggestive, however, that it could well be the other way around.

[13] "A Retrospect," *Literary Essays of Ezra Pound,* ed. with introduction by T. S. Eliot (New York: New Directions, 1968), p. 4.

[14] *Selected Essays of William Carlos Williams,* p. 35.

[15] *The Wine of the Puritans,* p. 128.

[16] *Ibid.,* p. 130.

[17] *The Ferment of Realism,* p. 297.

[18] Introduction, *Exiles and Emigrés: Studies in Modern Literature* (New York: Schocken Books, 1970).

[19] See John R. Harrison, *The Reactionaries: Yeats, Lewis, Pound, Eliot, Lawrence* (New York: Schocken Books, 1967).

[20] David Williams, "The Exile as Uncreator," *Mosaic,* 8 (Spring 1975), 5, 8-9, 14.

[21] Letter dd. 29 August 1904 in *Letters of James Joyce,* ed. Richard Ellmann (London: Faber & Faber, 1966), II, 89.

[22] *Ezra Pound* (New York: Funk & Wagnalls, 1960), p. 273.

[23] Richard Ellmann, *James Joyce* (New York: Oxford University

Press, 1959), p. 302.
    [24]"The Plunge," *Personae: The Collected Shorter Poems of Ezra Pound* (New York: New Directions, 1971), p. 70.

EZRA POUND'S ODYSSEY

Suffer, or enjoy, exile gladly.
Patria Mia

Why did so many writers leave their own countries during the first decades of this century to live in exile? Though expatriation was an international phenomenon, the largest contingent of exiles came from America. Much can be learned about the causes and consequences of exile by studying the life and work, including unpublished and new work, by and about a single American writer. Ezra Pound may seem a figure too exceptional, indeed unique, to be exemplary; his case, nevertheless, vividly dramatizes the advantages and disadvantages, the joys and sufferings of exile. Exile may be the result of necessity, will, or desire. It may be voluntary or involuntary. Pound's was both. Like Henry James and T. S. Eliot, he had negative reasons for leaving America and positive reasons for going to Europe. The United States at the turn of the century seemed to Pound an uncongenial place for a serious artist to live: "if you have any vital interest in arts and letters . . . you will sooner or later leave the country," Pound avers.[1] Like James, Pound had already visited and been ravished by Europe before he went there in 1908. When he left America, he did not intend going into permanent exile. Still, as a man in love with culture and tradition, and an artist athirst for the best in literature, music, painting, sculpture, and architecture—all, except the last, arts in which Pound exercised his own hand—Europe drew him irresistibly.

Pound at Home

Born in Hailey, Idaho in 1885, Pound moved with his family first to New York, then to Philadelphia. This was the beginning of the westerner's eastward migration; Pound remarked it was necessary to keep going east to keep one's mind alive. Pound was the only child of Homer and Isabel Pound; his relationship with his parents was so warm and admiring that friends of the family described it as a three-cornered mutual admiration society. Pound was educated at the University of Pennsylvania and attended Hamilton College. In 1906 he received an M.A. from the University of Pennsylvania and a fellowship to study in Spain the drama of Lope de Vega, the subject of a projected doctoral dissertation.[2] In the fall of 1907 Pound took a teaching position in Comparative Literature at Wabash College, Crawfordsville, Indiana. Within four months, he had been found *persona non grata* and dismissed. Wabash had already frowned on the poet as too bohemian before he found a penniless vaudeville actress stranded in a blizzard and sheltered her for a night in his rooms. The affair was innocent, but when Pound's cleaning ladies found the girl in his bed (the poet said he slept fully clothed on the floor), Pound's teaching career was at an end. This was unfortunate, for those who know Pound agree he was a born teacher. Pound, however, even prior to this incident, had conceived a lifelong contempt for the methods and mores of academe. Hereafter, American colleges and universities were for him "beaneries," filled with an apostolic succession of small-minded, unimaginative, plodding pedants and pedagogues. One can gain some notion of how lonely and alien Pound felt in the Indiana boondocks by reading an otherwise negligible early poem of his, "In Durance."

One could say, then, that Pound's abrupt dismissal from his teaching post, the closure of a career which would have given him time to write, was his most immediate reason for leaving the States. A more longstanding and weighty reason was what Pound saw as the impossibility of publishing his poetry in America. In "How I Began" he says that between 1903 and 1908 he succeeded in publishing only one poem.[3] In later years Pound would defend himself against charges of desertion made by poets who prided themselves on having stayed in America, such as William Carlos Williams, responding that, had he remained, he would have starved. This sounds hyperbolical, and in fact Pound's prolonged intimacy with hunger was *not* prevented by leaving his native shores. Pound's obsession with economics stemmed largely from his own precarious struggle to make a living. (Not until his sixties did Pound really make any money from his writing.) But Pound continued to think of the United

States as a country to live in which demanded a steady income. How was he to make a living here? He would probably have applied for another teaching post (he was to do so later at his parents' urging), but his disillusionment with the teaching profession was reinforced by his grim appraisal of the American literary scene. In *Patria Mia* he declares that there were in America when he left it no informed artistic taste or standards, no artists worthy of consideration, and no public for the arts. T. S. Eliot corroborates this verdict in his portrait of his colleague. The years 1900-14, as far as American poetry is concerned, were a blank: "there was no poet . . . who could have been of use to a beginner in 1908. The only recourse was to poetry of another age and to poetry of another language."[4] Pound accordingly plunged into Provençal poetry and Eliot into poetry of the French *fin-de-siecle.*

To study these, to unlock the whole thesaurus of western literary culture, how much better to be on the spot in Europe. On entering the University of Pennsylvania at the precocious age of fifteen, Pound had already defined his life's ambition:

> I resolved that at thirty I would know more about poetry than any man living, that I would know the dynamic content from the shell, that I would know what was accounted poetry everywhere, what part of poetry was "indestructible," what part could *not be lost* by translation, and . . . what effects were obtainable in *one* language only and were utterly incapable of being translated.
>
> In this search I learned more or less of nine languages. . . .[5]

At Pennsylvania and while "in exile" in upper New York State at Hamilton College, Pound had already launched himself on his life's project. Its maturing required the poet-scholar's removal from what he thought of as the cultural desert of the United States to the rich artistic treasury of Europe. To his parents Pound wrote, "Continued residence in America is . . . revolting to think of," and "you can't expect me seriously to consider America as a permanent place of abode." Already in Indiana, young Ezra was dreaming of Venice: "After 21 yrs . . . I can retire to Venice on half pay and live and loaf as I please," he writes his mother on nailing down the Wabash job.[6] Little did he realize his dream would be fulfilled less than a year later.

Pound as Odysseus

Traveling was for Pound a psychological imperative. Unlike T. S. Eliot, he never really settled permanently anywhere. Pound's temperament was nomadic; he wanted constantly to be on the move, with no more possessions than could be crammed into a single suitcase. From an early age he had been bitten by wanderlust, wishing to see many different places, men, and manners. Pound visualized himself as a contemporary Odysseus—*pollon d'anthropon iden*—or as a modern Dante in exile. Ezra Pound was born in exile. He felt himself an exile in America, both early and late. While imprisoned here from 1946-58, Pound called himself an exile in his own land. Wherever he was, Pound saw himself as voyager and outsider. His poems are peopled by and focus on wanderers, exiles, men far from home. "Have I a country at all?" he asks, and asks not self-pityingly but musingly, sometimes defiantly.[7] For Pound, even more than Eliot, was an internationalist. He disliked provincialism in literature and nationalism in politics. He wanted to be a citizen of the world at the center of things. Like Eliot, Pound was urban and metropolitan; he upheld the superiority of the city, as a center of civilization, to the country. (Indeed, Pound positively disliked the country.) His life was a long search for the ideal city which in *The Cantos* he calls Dioce.

T. S. Eliot said Pound always appeared to be a squatter, poised for flight. The phenomenon puzzled Eliot, for he himself had gone to Europe in search of roots, which he duly put down in England. He said of Pound, "I have never known a man, of any nationality, to live so long out of his native country without seeming to settle anywhere else." Eliot detected in Pound "a resistance against growing into any environment."[8] This is a shrewd diagnosis, for Pound had the tourist mentality, the desire continually to be visiting new places, seeing new sights, hearing new tongues, meeting new people. Richard Ellmann says of James Joyce (another writer who thought of himself as a Dante in exile) that he was a traveler by nature as well as necessity. Ellmann remarks: "When he had sufficiently complicated his life in one place, he preferred, instead of unraveling it, to move onto another."[9]   The remark has some applicability to Pound. There is an important difference, however, between these two writers-in-exile. Joyce's European odyssey appears to have left almost no mark on his work. Joyce had to leave Ireland to write about her, but his subject from first to last is Dublin. Dublin is the Ithaca from which he departed and to which, in imagination, he always returns. Whereas vivid memories of Pound's odyssey from Venice to London to Paris to Rapallo, then to the madhouse in Washington and back to Italy appear all through his work, particularly in the mental log of *The Cantos.* Pound's Ithaca became a paradisal city of the imagination, something like Yeats's Byzantium.

Pound in Venice

Why was Venice Pound's first port-of-call after leaving the United States? In fact, it was not; Pound first called at Gibraltar, having traveled there by cattleboat, with only $80 to his name, between January and February of 1908. He remained there some time, then made his way overland to Venice. Pound tells us in a brief, whimsical autobiography of his early years, *Indiscretions,* that he had a longstanding love affair with Venice. He first saw the miragelike, watery city at the age of thirteen, traveling there with his great aunt Frank. At seventeen he visited Venice again with his father. Pound's love for Venice embraced Northern Italy at large. Even after abandoning Venice for London, Pound wrote his father praising Northern Italy and declaring that, if he were not bound by the necessity of making a living, he would live there most of the time.[10] Pound was in Venice for about three months during the spring and summer of 1908, long enough to publish there his first volume of verse. *A Lume Spento* was printed at Pound's own expense in a very small edition. The poet had almost no money, lodged very cheaply at the Ponte San Vio, was often hungry, and, as he recalls in *Canto* 76, so little sure of himself or the future that he once contemplated throwing the proofs of his first book in the Grand Canal. But the desire grew on Pound to be at the center of things. Before World War I, the literary capital of the world was, as Pound put it, "the double city of London and Paris."

Pound's London Years

"I came to London with £3 knowing no one."[11]   Thus in-
auspiciously began the most important phase of Ezra Pound's
career.   Though not everyone agrees it was during the London
years, 1908-21, that Pound produced his own best work, he
did in this thirteen year period produce eleven volumes of
poetry, including *Personae, Ripostes, Cathay, Lustra,* and *Hugh
Selwyn Mauberley,* several important prose volumes, and an
enormous mass of writing for periodicals.   He served for several
years as literary agent for the *Egoist* and foreign correspondent
for *Poetry* and the *Little Review.*   In addition, as London's
literary impresario, Pound launched or promoted the careers of
T. S. Eliot, James Joyce, Robert Frost, William Carlos Williams,
H. D., Marianne Moore, Richard Aldington, and Wyndham Lewis,
among others.   He was one of the most discerning and helpful
critics and the most generous and indefatigable literary entrepreneur London had ever known.   His other activities in London included founding two literary movements, Imagism and
Vorticism, and, as Eliot put it, inventing Chinese poetry for
our time.   Pound was still comparatively a poor man when he
left London, but he knew and had helped in some way almost
everyone worth knowing or aiding in the world of the arts.
     One of Pound's foremost reasons for coming to London
was that he wanted to meet Yeats, whom he had probably heard
reading his poetry at the University of Pennsylvania in 1903.
The poets met, with happy results for Yeats's poetry and Pound's
career, about six months after Pound's arrival in London in
October 1908.[12]   During the winters of 1913-16, Pound was
Yeats's secretary and encouraged the older poet to renovate his
poetry, making it harder and clearer, more direct and colloquial.
(Yeats himself had powerfully influenced Pound's early poetry;
the Pre-Raphaelites and the poets of the nineties had influenced
them both.)   Pound also wanted to meet Swinburne and Ford
Madox Ford (then Ford Madox Hueffer).   Swinburne died in
April 1909, the month Pound's *Personae* appeared.   Ford became
a lifelong friend and influence.   Ford's ideals for prose—natural-
ness, objectivity, and precision—were those Pound cherished for
poetry.
     Pound's exhilaration at being in London, at the literary
heart of things, finds expression in his early letters home.   Indeed, Pound probably felt more at home in London during his

first years there, before 1913, than he had or ever was to feel anywhere else (except perhaps in Italy during his last years). In March 1909 Pound was writing his mother, "I seem to fit better here in London than anywhere else."[13] To William Carlos Williams (whom he met in his student days), Pound wrote exuberantly, "London, deah old Lundon, is the place for poesy." In May 1909 he reported proudly to Williams that he had been praised "by the greatest living poet. I am, after eight years' hammering against impenetrable adamant, become suddenly somewhat of a success." Yeats had praised *Personae*. Pound exulted, "There is no town like London to make one feel the vanity of all art except the highest."[14] In his poem "The Rest," addressed to beleaguered fellow artists left behind in America, Pound proclaims triumphantly: "I have weathered the storm, / I have beaten out my exile."

The signal achievements of Pound's career in London, the promise with which his life there began, occasion wonder that he should ever have left. What were the causes of Pound's disillusionment with the literary capital? They were many and interrelated. Pound still had difficulty getting published. Pound was an artistic revolutionary; his work was beyond his audience—both beyond its comprehension and ahead of its time. Indeed, Pound's audience steadily diminished as his career advanced. His prose Pound always regarded as "stopgap," but there were many more outlets for prose than for poetry, so he had to support himself by what he considered hackwork. Pound probably devoted more time and energy to promoting the work of fellow artists than he did to his own. He felt acutely, from 1914 on, that he needed more time for his own creative work, particularly for *The Cantos,* begun in 1915. In 1914 Pound acknowledged London was still the only sane place for a man of letters to live, but added, "I'm getting jolly tired of pushing other people's stuff."[15] While Pound was always friendly, generous, and self-sacrificing with those he respected among the literary *élite,* he was often savagely rude, arrogant, and contemptuous with editors, publishers, potential literary patrons, and the philistine public. Pound deplored Enlgish literary standards and literary magazines the more he learned of them. In *Patria Mia* Pound describes the English as a nation of amateurs in the arts; his own perfectionism and adherence to international standards of excellence were galled by a capital in which everybody's Uncle George or Aunt Lucy was writing a novel with his or her right hand while gardening or knitting with the left.

Pound's animus against the publishing world increased in virulence with each setback to his crusade for literary excellence. He nurtured a conspiracy theory about both the American and British publishing systems. In a letter written in the thirties, he retrospectively denounces "the Fleet St. ring" who made certain that Messrs. Joyce, Eliot, and Pound could be published only in little magazines.[16]   Pound's efficiency, generosity, and probity in fostering his friends' careers contrasts strikingly with his self-destructiveness in dealing with his own.[17] It is not surprising, given Pound's rudeness and intransigence, that we should find him writing Joyce at the beginning of 1916: "I have absolutely no connections in England that are any use."[18] By the end of 1919, Pound told John Quinn: "Have had my work turned down by about every editor in England and America. . . ."[19]

It is difficult to give a condensed account of Pound's tortuous relationship with literary magazines, but the attempt should be made, for it was largely due to his loss of publishing outlets between 1914 and 1919 that Pound left London. He served as *Poetry*'s foreign correspondent from that magazine's inception in 1912 until 1919; his final break with Harriet Monroe's journal came as a result of the academic furore created by his publication in *Poetry* of his *Homage to Sextus Propertius.* Pound also acted as literary agent for Harriet Shaw Weaver's *Egoist* from 1913 to 1919, a magazine he admired and with which Pound maintained amicable relations.   The New York patron of arts and letters, John Quinn, secured for Pound the foreign editorship of Margaret Anderson and Jane Heap's *Little Review,* from 1917 to 1919, at a salary of $750 (£150) per annum. This was Pound's first regular salary, but the lion's share of it went into procuring manuscripts.   When Pound lost his position with the *Little Review,* Eliot was able through Quinn to arrange for his appointment as foreign correspondent for the *Dial,* a position Pound held from 1920-23. (In Paris, Pound also briefly reassociated himself with the *Little Review.*) During Pound's tenure, all these magazines published brilliant work: he filled their pages with poetry by Yeats, Eliot, Frost, H. D., and Aldington, as well as his own; with fiction by Wyndham Lewis and James Joyce, and with criticism by himself, Eliot, and other members of the *avant garde.*   At Pound's instigation, the *Egoist* published Joyce's *A Portrait of the Artist as a Young Man,* and the *Little Review* published his *Ulysses* (until it was suppressed in the summer of 1920). Pound also contributed to the *Atheneum*, BLAST, the *Criterion*, the *English Review*, the *Fortnightly Review*, *Future*, *Others*, *Outlook*, *Poetry & Drama*, *Poetry Review*, and the *Quarterly Review of Literature*. His financial mainstay was A. R. Orage's *New Age*, for which he wrote literary, musical, and art criticism and economic articles. Biographers affirm that by 1919 Pound had antagonized all London's editors except Orage. Pound said so himself. He was either fired by the other journals or severed himself from them in disgust at their editorial policies. Orage wrote, in the issue of *The New Age* in which Pound published his "last will and testament" on leaving London, that despite all Pound had done for English letters, he had made many more enemies than friends. "Much of the press has deliberately closed by cabal to him; his books have for some time been ignored or written down; and he himself has been compelled to live on much less that would support a navvy."[20] In Pound's poetic "last will and testament" to London, *Hugh Selwyn Mauberley*, he alienated most of his English readers beyond recall. Pound would have had to be superhuman not to be embittered by his difficulties in an unremitting struggle to publish the best work, but it is plain that he was his own worst enemy and that, having once been victimized, he continued to victimize himself.

The personality which raised Pound to eminence only to plunge him into depths of ignominy was one of extraordinary complexity, probably best summed up by his lifelong friend, William Carlos Williams. Williams writes of Pound: "not one person in a thousand likes him, and a great many people detest him and why? Because he is so darned full of conceits and affection. He is really a brilliant talker and thinker but delights in making himself . . . a laughing boor. His friends must be all patience in order to find him out and even then you must not let him know it, for he will immediately put on some artificial mood and be really unbearable. It is too bad, for he loves to be liked, but there is some quality in him which makes him too proud to try to please people."[21] Pound's intimates agree that under a prickly and forbidding exterior he had a warm heart, but many who met Pound, particularly in England, were repelled by his histrionic poses and posturings, his flaunted eccentricity, and what seemed a swaggering arrogance. Wyndham Lewis recalls watching Pound's first entry into English society.

He says Pound had no luck with the English from the start, for they instinctively resented his desire to impress, being determined not to be impressed, particularly by an American. Lewis says Pound was always out of his element in England, that his bohemianism was much more at home in France, and that, though Pound knew England well, he never came to terms with it.[22]

Pound's very appearance must have caused English society to bristle. He got himself up to look like an Elizabethan rake. The flamboyance of his tall, lanky frame and sharp features (a leonine mane of red-blond hair and jutting beard, piercing blue-green eyes) were set off by costumes sometimes prompted by poverty as much as a pronounced taste for the exotic. Pound's clothes were of outlandish cut, cloth, and color, and worn with odd accessories. He strode about town flourishing a malacca cane and sporting a broad-brimmed hat, one gold earring, flowing handpainted tie, violent colored shirt, and trousers seemingly made of green billiard cloth. Pound's cocky self-assurance, his unshakable conviction of the absolute rightness of his opinions, his habit, as Gertrude Stein put it, of lecturing everyone as though he were a "village explainer" provoked in many Englishmen the desire to take his parakeet down a peg. Pound made enemies much more easily than he made friends. Yet Lewis testifies to a kind of impersonality in Pound which one senses if one studies his poetry and his life. "No envy of the individual attached to the work. I have never known a person less troubled by personal feelings. This probably it is that has helped to make Pound that odd figure—the great poet and great impresario at one and the same time."[23]

Though it is not the popular view of Pound, it would be true to call him a pacifist. He loathed war. (His family had been Quakers.) He deplored nationalism. His perspective, in politics as in poetry, was international. In November 1914 Pound foresaw that World War I would bring about the disintegration of the British Empire and that it was the beginning of the end of British civilization. Pound volunteered but was found unfit for service. Friends were mobilized; London became an intellectual wasteland in their absence. Some of Pound's most brilliant friends died in the trenches: T. E. Hulme the philosopher and Gaudier-Brzeska the sculptor.

> There died a myriad,
> And of the best, among them,
> For an old bitch gone in the teeth,
> For a botched civilization,
>
> Charm, smiling at the good mouth,
> Quick eyes gone under earth's lid,
>
> For two gross of broken statues,
> For a few thousand battered books.

When the survivors returned, London, as Pound had foreseen, was no longer a metropolis with a thriving literary life but a necropolis. The scene is depicted, with grotesque and diabolical hyperbole, in Pound's Hell Cantos.

During the war it was particularly difficult to make a living by one's pen, but Pound toiled away, waging his war of letters in straitened and constricting circumstances. The wanderer in him chafed at confinement; in 1917 he was already looking forward to going to Paris when war ended. Deeply disillusioned with one half of the western world's literary capital, he would try his fortunes in the other. Pound had fallen out of love with London. The longed-for armistice ushered in a period of austerity, weariness, cynicism, and despair. Those who had fought at the front were alienated from those who had not.

> These fought in any case,
> and some believing,
>   pro domo, in any case. . .
> . . . .
> Died some, pro patria,
>   non "dulce" non "et decor". . .
> walked eye-deep in hell
> believing in old men's lies, then unbelieving
> come home, home to a lie,
> home to many deceits,
> home to old lies and new infamy;
> usury age-old and age-thick
> and liars in public places.[24]

Their bodies battered, nerves shattered, and spirits crippled, the returning soldiers could scarcely recognize the country or cause for which they had fought. Unemployment was widespread, nor was this problem to be solved in a decade. "England under a curse" is a refrain that sounds through Pound's letters and valedictory articles. In 1920 Pound wrote Williams that the only intellectual life to be found in England was what took place in his own room.[25]

Pound prepared to leave and Eliot to take over as London's literary dictator. Richard Aldington has compared their two careers:

> Tom Eliot's career in England had been exactly the reverse of Ezra's. Ezra started out in a time of peace and prosperity with everything in his favor, and muffed his chances of becoming literary dictator of London—to which he undoubtedly aspired—by his own conceit, folly, and bad manners. Eliot started in the enormous confusion of war and post-war England, handicapped in every way. Yet by merit, tact, prudence, and pertinacity he succeeded in doing what no other American has ever done—imposing his personality, taste, and . . . opinions on literary England.[26]

While Aldington is right about the personalities of the two poets, to say that Eliot's career was the exact reverse of Pound's is simplistic. Though Pound came to London before the war, there was precious little peace or prosperity in his first years there—or indeed in his entire life. Aldington neglects to say that Pound *helped* Eliot to his place. When Eliot came to London at the outbreak of war, Pound published poems of his that had been lying in a desk drawer for three years. Pound watched over Eliot's career with great solicitude. He contributed himself and urged others' contributions to subsidize Eliot so that he would not have to drudge in Lloyds Bank. (To this end, Pound even offered to forego his own salary from the *Dial.*) Pound provided Eliot with valuable literary contacts. For Eliot Pound remained to the end *"il miglior fabbro,"* the better craftsman. In Eliot's portrait of Pound, he pays tribute to Pound's unfailing generosity and to the soundness of his literary judgment, while acknowledging his friend to be a very fallible judge of men. Pound's most important and lasting contribution to literature, says Eliot, is that he created the conditions in which modern poetry could come into being on both sides of the Atlantic.[27]

Pound in Paris

What better and more obvious place for Pound to go, after exhausting London, than Paris? Paris in the twenties was a home away from home for a whole colony of artists-in-exile. For Ezra Pound, desirous of being at the center, it was, at the time, the only place to be. Nevertheless, Pound's removal to Paris was preceded by a period of uncertainty about his work and his future. For over a year, during 1919 and 1920, he traveled back and forth between England and the continent. In 1919 he took his wife for a war-deferred honeymoon to his beloved Provence. He was there again and in Northern Italy the following year. The fateful meeting between Pound and Joyce took place at Sirmione in June 1920. Joyce found Pound (despite radical uncertainties about his own career) very helpful in furthering Joyce's; he called Pound "a miracle of ebulliency, gusto, and help," and "a large bundle of unpredictable electricity."[28] Pound persuaded Joyce to leave Trieste for Paris, which Joyce did a month later. Pound was visiting Paris when the Joyces arrived; he found them an apartment in the rue de l'université and helped them move in. It was not until December 1920, however, that Pound decided to move permanently to Paris himself; before doing so, he went to the Riviera. In April 1921 the Pounds were living in the rue des Sts. Pères; in December of that year they had moved to the studio they were to occupy throughout Pound's Parisian sojourn, 70 bis rue Notre Dame des Champs.

Pound's desire to be surrounded by interesting people was fulfilled in Paris. He made new friends and artistic discoveries and was visited by old ones. With Gertrude Stein he did not hit it off, but Paris was large enough to contain them both. Pound continued to be an impresario and a Renaissance man, enlarging the scope of his talents. Still writer, critic, translator, editor, and promoter, he also made forays into music, composing an opera on Villon, and into sculpture. He cooked and carpentered, fenced, boxed, and played tennis. He met and fostered the careers of Hemingway, Cummings, George Antheil, and Constantin Brancusi, as well as Joyce. Ford Madox Ford had moved to Paris and, with Quinn's backing, set up the *transatlantic review.* Pound seemed, to old friends who visited him in Paris, happier there than in London, more in his element. Among his visitors were Eliot, Lewis, Williams, Harriet Monroe, and Margaret Anderson. Pound was better off than he had been in London, chiefly

because of the salary paid by the *Dial* and the low cost of living
in Paris. One could live well in Paris in the twenties for very
little. (Exchange rates were then five francs to the dollar and
five dollars to the pound.) Nevertheless, Pound was still experiencing difficulty making a living.

In a book called *Les Années Vingt,* William Bird exclaims:
"*Le premier évènement d'importance pour la littérature améri-
caine des années 20 fut l'émigration d'Ezra Pound de Londres à
Paris.*"[29] Pound became one of the literary totems of the American expatriate colony in Paris. What were the accomplishments
of his Paris years? His achievements as a literary entrepreneur far
surpassed his achievements as a writer. In December 1917 Pound
received the first pages of *Ulysses* from Joyce. For three years,
from 1917 through 1921, he received successive chapters and
saw them into print in the *Little Review.* To Pound *Ulysses,* that
"epoch-making report on the state of the human mind in the
twentieth century," signaled the beginning of a new, non-Chris-
tian era. He modestly named it "the Pound Era" and dated it
from his thirty-sixth birthday, October 30, 1921, the date on
which Joyce finished *Ulysses.* *Ulysses* exerted a considerable
influence on Pound's own work-in-progress, *The Cantos.* It was
one of the factors impelling Pound to enlarge his subject matter
and to grapple with history, society, economics, and politics in
poetry. *Ulysses* appeared in book form, published by Sylvia
Beach's Shakespeare & Company, in February 1922. In the fall
of that year another bombshell burst on the literary world with
Eliot's *The Waste Land.* Pound had acted as midwife to Eliot's
poem—those familiar with the facsimile edition know how well,
and how deserved was Eliot's praise of Pound's bluepenciling.
The Waste Land too made a deep impression on its editor. It
prompted dissatisfaction with his own poetry, which now seemed
to Pound too precious and old-fashioned. When he first encountered Eliot, what most impressed him was that Eliot had
"modernized" himself. Pound was constantly trying to modern-
ize his poetry but needed other poets to show him how. So he
writes Eliot in year one of the new era: "Complimenti. . . . I am
wracked by the seaven jealousies, and cogitating an excuse for
always exuding my deformative secretions in my own stuff, and
never getting an outline. I go into nacre and objects d'art." But
Pound concludes by rejoicing at this latest arrival in the world of
letters: "It is after all a grrreat littttttterary period."[30] For himself, Pound's Paris years were not nearly so productive as his

London years. He translated Rémy de Gourmont's *The Natural Philosophy of Love* and edited a series of books for Williams Bird's Three Mountains Press, which included Hemingway's *In Our Time*. And he chafed to make greater inroads on his own "leviathanically long poem," *The Cantos*, the first sixteen of which were printed in a de luxe edition by Three Mountains Press in 1925.

One of Pound's chief reasons for leaving Paris was that he needed more time to devote to *The Cantos*, which he already planned would number over a hundred and which he estimated would require another forty years to complete. By 1922 Pound was restless. The Paris years seem to have made less impression on him than his London ones. They have left little trace in *The Cantos*. "There is a hint of frenzy in the Paris records and memoirs," remarks a biographer, and adds that Pound seems to have been "running from something—himself, most probably."[31] In 1923 Pound's health broke down; he had two or three bouts with appendicitis before recovering in 1924. He began to find Paris enervating. He was fired from the *Dial*. An issue on exile, conceived by Pound, appeared in May 1923, but Pound is not represented in it. After his dismissal, Pound appears for the first time to be at his wits' end. To a friend he confessed, "I don't know where to go next."[32] How low his spirits had sunk appears by his even considering returning to the United States, but he felt his last link with America had been severed. Once more, as he had before leaving London for his next place of exile, Pound underwent a period of great restlessness and uncertainty. In 1923 the Pounds were shuttling back and forth between France and Italy looking for a place to settle. That Dorothy disliked Paris as much as she loved Italy probably influenced their change of domicile. Pound's own health prompted him to seek a more permanent place in the sun of the Italian Riviera.

Pound in Rapallo

Pound seems to have chosen Rapallo as the place of his last and longest exile because of its beauty, climate, and cheapness.[33] That it was, compared with London and Paris, off the beaten track was one of its greatest attractions, for Pound wanted to settle down to his own creative work. Against Ford's contention that France was the last, best hope of civilization after the First World War, Pound upheld Italy, saying she had civilized Europe twice and might do so a third time. Pound was attracted by Italian *virtù* and what he thought would be a *Rinascimento* under Mussolini. Rapallo drew the poet with more immediately vivid and sensuous charms. Life here was simpler and pleasanter than it had been in Paris. Pound had always been afraid of catching colds, and he and Dorothy both disliked cold, wet climates. Rapallo's climate was ideal. Yeats compared Rapallo to the little town Keats describes in his "Ode on a Grecian Urn."[34] In the twenties Rapallo's beach was still unfrequented; grand hotels had not yet sprung up, each guarding with a paraphernalia of bathing cabins, beach chairs, and umbrellas a strip of sand to which access could be had only for a fee. There was neither marina nor casino—just the sparkling Mediterranean spread beneath olive crowned hills.

The move to Rapallo also meant a change in mental climate or atmosphere for Pound. It marks a division in Pound's life, the end of one phase of his career and the beginning of another. No longer was he a literary impresario; to a considerable extent, Pound exchanged his involvement in literary affairs for an embroilment in economics and politics. While forging ahead with *The Cantos,* and finally editing his own magazine, *Exile* (which ran, however, to only four issues in 1927-28), Pound also produced a flood of periodical articles, mostly on economics. Between 1928 and 1942 Pound wrote tens of thousands of letters, some of them to important public figures, in an urgent attempt to save civilization and forestall World War II.[35] Pound held that poets are "the antennae of the race"; his antennae told him the Peace of Versailles would prove only a truce. The superpowers were rearming at the instigation, as he saw it, of international banking interests. A man of grandiose ambitions and high ideals, always a believer in simple solutions to complex problems, Pound had wanted before World War I to found a new civilization; after it, he wanted to save the old one and appointed himself civilization's savior. At the very least, he determined to save some fragment of civilization on the Mediterranean. Pound turned Rapallo into a cultural center; he became a musical impresario, initiating a series of concerts devoted to fine but little known composers and to the lesser known works of great composers. In Rapallo he received a small band of disciples comprising both poets and students of economics. Pound's publications during his Rapallo years were a mixture of literature and economics. He composed more than half *The Cantos* there. He expanded *How to Read* into his *ABC of Reading* (1934). He also published an *ABC of Economics* in 1933, *Jefferson and/or Mussolini* in 1935, and his *Guide to Kulchur* in 1938. This by no means exhausts the list of Pound's writings while in Rapallo.

Rapallo complicated Pound's personal life. Olga Rudge, the American violinist whom he had first heard play in London, became Pound's mistress and in July 1925 gave birth to an illegitimate daughter, Mary. Mary was consigned to a wetnurse and foster mother in Gais, in the Italian Tyrol. In September 1926 Dorothy, Pound's wife, gave birth to his son, Omar. Omar was sent to London to be brought up by the Shakespears, Dorothy's parents. His mother would visit Omar every summer for several months, at which time Pound would move to Olga Rudge's house in Venice to be with Olga and Mary. He took a hand in Mary's education, very little in Omar's. Olga Rudge also had a small cottage in the hills above Rapallo, in Sant' Ambrogio. While in Rapallo, Pound would hustle back and forth between his seafront home with Dorothy (Via Marsala 12) and Olga's Casa Sessanta in the hills. Though the two women were compelled to confront each other periodically, there was no communication between them until the war.[36]

In spring 1944 the Germans requisitioned Pound's house in the Via Marsala and he and Dorothy were driven to seek shelter with Olga in Sant' Ambrogio. At this time Pound's assets were frozen and the three were forced to live in a very strained, straitened, and unhappy *ménage-à-trois*. Meanwhile, Homer and Isabel Pound had retired to Rapallo at Pound's urging. (Both Pound's parents were to die in Italy. His father's last illness was one of the difficulties militating against Pound's return to the United States during the war, as was his inability to secure clearance papers for his daughter.) In Rapallo, then, Pound became something of a paterfamilias, surrounded by parents, wife, mistress, and a child. His rather strange domestic arrangements do suggest Pound put down deeper roots in Rapallo than elsewhere. He must have felt at home there, for he returned to spend his last years in Rapallo and Venice, as he had these twenty-one years of his exile between 1924 and 1945. Pound's fidelity to Rapallo contrasts strongly with his attitude to his other places of exile. He had settled enthusiastically in London and Paris, but repudiated both cities and nations on leaving them.

In historical perspective, the effects of Pound's exile in Rapallo seem to have been pernicious. For it was in Rapallo that Pound started down the path that was to lead to the cage in the detention center at Pisa and the madhouse of St. Elizabeth's in Washington. Rapallo, because it was a relatively isolated refuge, confirmed Pound in his eccentricities and obsessions. He no longer had the benefit of intellectual give-and-take with equals. Apart from Yeats and other old artist friends who visited him, those who came to call on Pound were mostly youngsters eager to sit in adulation at the feet of *il maestro* and to lap up his opinions on poetry and economics. Without a sounding board against which to try his ideas, or opposition to challenge them, they hardened into *idées fixes.* Pound became hypnotized by his self-appointed mission to save Europe, and in the process lost himself.

Pound's Nekuia or Descent into Hell

The story of Pound's broadcasts, arrest, detention at Pisa, treason trial, and imprisonment in St. Elizabeth's mental hospital has been told so often that summary and brief comment will suffice here. It is not generally known that Pound began broadcasting his economic theories as early as 1935.[37] In 1939 Pound made a trip to the United States in the hope of preventing war. He wanted to talk to President Roosevelt, as he had talked to Mussolini in 1933, but was denied access to the President. Pound returned to Italy disappointed. In the late thirties he had seriously considered returning to America permanently. During the war he tried to return twice but was prevented. Pound was declared a traitor for his regular broadcasts to the American people over Rome Radio between 1941 and 1943. He suspended his broadcasts after Pearl Harbor but resumed them a few weeks later. The broadcasts were initially intended to keep the United States out of the war. They were violent, vituperative, sometimes obscene, and consistently incoherent in their praise of fascism, denunciation of Allied leaders and policies, and recurrent anti-Semitism. Hearing or reading them is enough to make one writhe with shame for Pound. But Pound was not in fact a fascist, and he was an anti-Semite in theory rather than practice. He detested the Jews as a race because he associated them with usury; nonetheless, as he used to point out (in a lapse into cliché), some of his best friends were Jews. Pound was not a traitor. He never considered himself anything but an American, and proud of it. His real quarrel with America was that she was not American enough, unfaithful to her Constitution and the ideals of her Founding Fathers, untrue to her native genius. Pound refused to consider giving up his citizenship, which he would have done had he really been a fascist traitor. His broadcasts, violently irrational and incoherent as they are, were the misguided effort of a deeply disturbed mind to communicate its firmly held convictions to a civilization in the throes of self-destruction. The charge that Pound made these broadcasts for money is false, although it is true that his family was dependent on what he could earn by writing articles and making speeches, since his royalties had been frozen by the Italian Government, which ironically regarded Pound as an enemy alien.

Pound was seized by Italian Partisans and gave himself up to the U. S. authorities in Genoa in May 1945. For six months he was held at the Disciplinary Training Center in Pisa, along with murderers, rapists, thieves, and all the delinquent flotsam of the U. S. Army thereabouts. Pound was first placed in solitary confinement in a heavily reinforced "gorilla cage" for several weeks, until he collapsed. He was then removed to a tent in the medical compound. His family were not informed where he was nor permitted to visit him until October 1945. In November he was flown to Washington to stand trial for treason in January 1946. On February 13, 1946 psychiatrists certified he was insane and unfit to defend himself. He was then consigned to the "hellhole" at St. Elizabeth's, a windowless ward for criminal lunatics; Pound was the only inmate not in a straitjacket. After eighteen months without seeing daylight, Pound was removed to a regular ward.

With the benefit of hindsight one may say that, if Pound was ever insane, it was only intermittently. At Pisa under brutal, indeed bestial conditions, Pound studied Confucius and composed most of the beautiful *Pisan Cantos,* incomparably the finest lyric sequence in *The Cantos.* In St. Elizabeth's Pound read continuously, received many visitors, talked and wrote. His Paradiso, the *Rock-Drill* and *Thrones* sections of *The Cantos,* came out of an Inferno. These were the years Pound referred to as years of being an exile in his own country, confined in a madhouse within the larger madhouse of the United States of America. To be an exile implies mental alienation, means feeling habitually alien to one's environment. At Pisa and in Washington, Pound's profound sense of not belonging where he was helped to preserve his sanity and perhaps his life. Friends and admirers who visited him at St. Elizabeth's marveled at Pound's composure, cooped up as he was with lunatics and deprived of those sensuous stimuli which are a poet's essential nutriment. Michael Reck, who visited Pound in the mental hospital over a period of seven years, said that he kept alive on his memories.

> nothing matters but the quality
> of the affection -
> in the end - that has carved the trace in the mind
> dove sta memoria.[38]

William Carlos Williams was amazed by Pound's serenity and impassivity in face of his stygian surroundings.[39] Pound's daughter, visiting him in 1953, was as appalled by his companions as by his physical surroundings; she believed her father dared not dwell on the possibility of gaining his freedom for fear of going mad.[40] Instead he kept his mind constantly occupied with large, impersonal economic, social, and political issues.

Nostos or the End of Pound's Odyssey

On his release from St. Elizabeth's, almost thirteen years to the day after his surrender in Genoa, Pound returned to Italy. Having been declared of unsound mind, he was released in custody of his wife and his secretary. For six months he stayed with his daughter and son-in-law, Mary and Boris de Rachewiltz, and his grandchildren at Brunnenberg in the Southern Tyrol. The Rachewiltzes live in a medieval castle which they turned, in anticipation of Pound's return, into a museum housing his manuscripts and most treasured possessions. But Pound found the height of Schloss Brunnenberg oppressive. In 1959 he returned to Rapallo, his Ithaca, spending summers there and the remainder of the year in Olga Rudge's house in Venice. Sometime after a serious illness in 1959, Pound separated from his faithful wife who had visited him every day while he was confined in St. Elizabeth's. Olga Rudge took care of Pound during the sixties until his death in November 1972. The poet aged with startling suddenness, lapsing from polyglot loquacity into a silence he rarely broke. Pound's silence and the few remarks he made publicly indicate that he was overcome with remorse, that many of his old convictions had been shattered, that he was profoundly disillusioned with his own mental capacity and even, perhaps, with the power of words. His friend Old Billyum, William Butler Yeats, had declared, "Words alone are certain good." Pound was no longer convinced. He appears to have ceased writing at the time of his illness; his last *Cantos* (together with fragments, they number the projected hundred and twenty) were written in the late fifties. The last one begins, "I have tried to write Paradise," and ends: "Let the Gods forgive what I have made / Let those I love try to forgive what I have made." Pound described himself as a man on whose head all Europe had fallen. In one of his last interviews he said that, having been certain all his life of many things, he was left at the end with "only the certainty of my incertitude."[41]

An American in Exile

Although Pound spent sixty-four years in exile from his homeland, and twelve years as an exile within it, he remained an American all his life. Even his speech—and he knew nine languages, of which he spoke five fluently—had a distinctly American twang, though overlaid with strange accents and cosmopolitan exclamations. Pound never thought of himself as anything but an American. In *Patria Mia* he says that "it would be about as easy for an American to become a Chinaman or a Hindoo as for him to acquire an Englishness, or a Frenchness, or a Europeanness that is more than half a skin deep."[42] In the same work and throughout his life, Pound showed an abiding interest in America, a great longing for an American Renaissance which, he was sure, would make the Italian *Rinascimento* look like a tempest in a teapot. On his own testimony, Pound felt increasingly American as he grew older. He admired the tough, energetic, pioneering temperament of men like his grandfather, Thaddeus Coleman Pound, who was a lumberjack and railroader before he became a Congressman. Pound said he himself had probably never outlived the frontier.[43] It was his American restlessness, energy, and his aspiration after the highest possible international standards that drove Pound to Europe. In London and Paris he constituted himself an advance guard and established a beachhead for American poets and American poetry. No one promoted American poetry as tirelessly as Pound. Hence his quarrel with William Carlos Williams when Williams pronounced him "the best enemy United States verse had." Williams was spokesman for those American poets who stayed put, against the "exotics"—like Pound and Eliot—who had chosen as models the foreign and bygone and who had gone abroad. As Eliot remarked of Henry James, however, "It is only an American who can choose to be a European." In his controversy with Williams, Pound insisted he was more American than Williams and, for that very reason, had to leave the country. (Pound prided himself that his ancestors on both sides had been among the first English colonists; Williams was of mixed English-Spanish parentage.) Pound argues there is a virus in America to which Williams, with his mixed blood, was immune, while he and Eliot had to escape it. This virus Pound associates with abstract ideation, with a tendency toward propaganda and confusion of public with private life, with a "thin logical faculty" (remarkable self-insight), and perhaps with puritanism.[44] Not only did America not offer Pound the kind of intellectual sustenance he needed as a poet, he feared that what sustenance America did offer would be such as to turn him into a propagandist and pamphleteer rather than a poet. Italy seems to have produced the same result; it was not so much the place as the time and the worldwide depression that did it, and most of Pound's propaganda was directed to America, intended on her behalf.

Pound's intimates also testify to his Americanness. To his wife he always seemed "quintessentially American." The English uniformly so regarded him. Eliot they finally accepted as one themselves, but Pound, in Eliot's and others' eyes, was a restless bird of passage. To Mary Colum he appeared, despite his Renaissance head and beard, every inch a Midwestern professor![45] Michael Reck found him both "rustic and cosmopolitan," a mélange of American and European. He cites Archibald MacLeish's remark that Pound's internationalism is typically American. A European, MacLeish said, is satisfied with a single culture; only an American would spend his life sampling different cultures, then collecting and commemorating the samples, as Pound did: "because Pound is so international, he is so American."[46]

One cannot help remarking how, throughout the first quarter of the century, American artists hungry for beauty, culture, and pleasure emigrated or spent an important part of their careers in Europe—the movement had begun in the nineteenth century. It was then a movement from the margins to the center —as George Steiner so beautifully expresses it, "a nostalgic, obsessed voyage through the museum of high culture just before closing time . . . a final race through the stacks before the illiterates and the bookburners take over."[47] Pound describes in "How I Began" with what zest he went about London, recreating the lives of his favorite poets from study of their work, houses, relics, and surviving relatives and friends. "This, perhaps means little to a Londoner, but it is good fun if you have grown up regarding such things as about as distant as Ghengis Kahn or the days of Lope de Vega."[48]   Steiner observes, "Seen in this way, the marginal origins of Pound, Eliot, and Joyce, their upbringing on the frontier of the declining cultural imperium, make beautiful sense: only a man from Idaho or St. Louis would bring such indefatigable zest, such 'tourist passion' to the job of discovering and cataloguing the old spendors of . . . Europe. . . ."[49]

Pound was born and lived almost all his life in exile. Exile is of course spiritual before it becomes physical, and Pound's was metaphysical as much as physical. Already while living in America, Pound really inhabited a country of the imagination. Venice, London, Paris, and Rapallo approximated more closely to his desires, but he never found his ideal city, his heart's home, and his initial ravishment with Europe was not his final feeling. In the early sixties, Pound observed that Europe was no longer the center of civilization and referred to himself as "the last American living the tragedy of Europe."[50]   Still it is beautiful and somehow fitting that Pound should have ended where he began his poetic career. He died in Venice just after his eighty-seventh birthday. His coffin was borne by gondola to the island of San Michele. Paradise, Pound knew, is not terrestrial but a state of mind. For all that, he assures us that it is real, not artificial. It is to be found, in fleeting glimpses, in his poems.

NOTES

[1] Ezra Pound, *Patria Mia* (Chicago: Ralph Fletcher Seymour, 1950), p. 37.

[2] The dissertation was never completed, though the research Pound did for it was incorporated in *The Spirit of Romance.*

[3] Originally published in *T. P's Weekly,* June 6, 1913, reprinted in *Ezra Pound: A Collection of Criticism,* ed. Grace Schulman, Contemporary Studies in Literature (New York: McGraw-Hill, 1974), p. 23.

Pound's biographer Noel Stock says Pound tried unsuccessfully to publish about forty poems before he left the United States. *The Life of Ezra Pound* (New York: Pantheon, 1970), p. 45.

[4] T. S. Eliot, "Ezra Pound," *Poetry,* 68 (September 1946), 326.

[5] "How I Began," *Ezra Pound,* ed. Grace Schulman, pp. 24-25.

[6] Unpublished letters, nos. 146, 148 & 72 dated January 20 & 31, 1910 and August 1907, respectively, to Isabel Pound in the Beinecke Collection of Yale University Library. I am indebted to the Beinecke Library and to the Trustees of the Ezra Pound Literary Property Trust for permission to quote from these letters, which are typescripts of correspondence gathered by D. D. Paige, but not included in his *Selected Letters of Ezra Pound, 1907-41.*

[7] Letter no. 170, *Selected Letters of Ezra Pound, 1907-41,* ed. D. D. Paige (New York: New Directions, 1971), p. 159. Consider, among others, the poems "Cino," "Exile's Letter," *The Seafarer* and, of course, *The Cantos.* Other poems such as "In Durance" and "The Plunge" testify to Pound's sense of alienation from his homeland or his longing to travel.

[8] "Ezra Pound," 327.

[9] Richard Ellmann, *James Joyce* (New York: Oxford University Press, 1959), p. 189.

[10] Unpublished letter no. 167 dd. April 10, 1910. Pound's "autobiography" is reprinted in his *Pavannes & Divagations* (Norfolk, Connecticut: New Directions, 1958).

[11] "How I Began," *Ezra Pound,* ed. Grace Schulman, p. 24.

[12] It is impossible to date Pound's arrival exactly, but Patricia Hutchins in *Ezra Pound's Kensington* (London: Faber & Faber, 1965), p. 49 notes Pound applied for a British Museum reading card early in October.

[13] Unpublished letter no. 104 dd. March 15, 1909.

[14] Letters nos. 3 & 4, *Selected Letters,* pp. 7-8.

[15] Letter no. 40 to Amy Lowell, *Selected Letters,* p. 33.

[16] Letter no. 252, *Selected Letters,* pp. 239-40.

[17] A letter to the editor of the *Saturday Review* shows how extremely abrasive Pound could be and how he could turn a potential benefactor into

an enemy for life. This magazine approached Pound to choose a poem of his for inclusion in an anthology it was sponsoring, for which he would be well paid. Pound replied that the *Saturday Review* had done nothing but pour poison in America's ear for years past. "The foetor of the *Saturday Review*'s critical effort to uphold the almost-good and the not-quite-dead. . . . How the deuce do you expect me to swallow all that for the sake of a small sum of money?" Letter no. 258 to Wm. Rose Benet, *Selected Letters*, p. 244.

[18] *Pound/Joyce: The Letters of Ezra Pound to James Joyce, With Pound's Essays on Joyce*, ed. with commentary by Forrest Read (New York: New Directions, 1970), p. 61.

[19] Letter no. 162, *Selected Letters*, p. 151.

[20] A. R. Orage, "Readers and Writers," *The New Age*, 28 (January 13, 1921), 126.

[21] William Carlos Williams, *Selected Letters*, ed. with introduction by John C. Thirlwall (New York: McDowell, Obolensky, 1957), p. 6.

[22] Wyndham Lewis, *Blasting & Bombardiering* (Berkeley: University of California Press, 1967), pp. 274 & 276.

[23] "Ezra: The Portrait of a Personality," *Quarterly Review of Literature*, 5 (December 1949), 144.

[24] *Hugh Selwyn Mauberley*, IV & V.

[25] Letter no. 170, *Selected Letters*, p. 158.

[26] Richard Aldington, *Life for Life's Sake* (New York: Viking, 1941), p. 217.

[27] T. S. Eliot, "Ezra Pound," *Poetry*, 68 (September 1946), 328 & 330.

[28] Herbert Gorman, *James Joyce* (New York: Farrar & Rinehart, 1939), p. 272.

[29] Cited by Charles Norman, *Ezra Pound* (New York: Funk & Wagnalls, 1960), p. 241.

[30] Letter no. 181, *Selected Letters*, pp. 169-70.

[31] Charles Norman, *Ezra Pound*, p. 273.

[32] Letter no. 195 to Kate Buss dd. May 12, 1923, *Selected Letters*, p. 186.

[33] There is disagreement as to when Pound discovered Rapallo and settled there. Michael Reck says a friend discovered this gem of a small seaside town on the Riviera di Levante, praised it to Ezra, and so the Pounds went to see it for themselves. *Ezra Pound: A Close-Up* (New York: McGraw-Hill, 1967), p. 48. Norman says Pound was already visiting Rapallo in 1922 (*Ezra Pound*, p. 258). Eustace Mullins declares Pound discovered Rapallo on a trip to Italy with the Hemingways in 1923, when he and Hemingway explored the battlefields of Piombino and Ortebello, reliving Malatesta's

campaigns. *This Difficult Individual: Ezra Pound* (New York: Fleet Publishing, 1961), p. 146. See also Carlos Baker, *Hemingway: The Writer as Artist* (Princeton: Princeton University Press, 1956), p. 18. Noel Stock says Pound left Paris for Rapallo on October 24, 1924—*The Life of Ezra Pound,* p. 256. Unpublished letters to his parents show that, although Pound was in Rapallo as early as January 1923, by October 1924 he still was not sure he wanted to settle there permanently. By November, however, the decision was made and Pound made arrangements to get rid of his Paris apartment. In Rapallo the Pounds lived at Via Marsala 12.

[34] W. B. Yeats, *A Packet for Ezra Pound* (Dublin: Cuala Press, 1929), p. 1.

[35] Noel Stock in *Reading the Cantos: The Study of Meaning in Ezra Pound* (New York: Pantheon, 1966), pp. 36-38, says that between 1933 and 1937 alone Pound wrote 400 articles! See also Noel Stock's *Poet in Exile: Ezra Pound* (Manchester: Manchester University Press, 1964), p. 146.

[36] According to Pound's daughter, not until she was eighteen did she learn from her father that there *was* a Mrs. Pound! Mary de Rachewiltz, *Discretions* (Boston, Mass.: Little, Brown, 1971), p. 187.

[37] See Alan Levy, "Ezra Pound's Voice of Silence," *New York Times Magazine,* January 9, 1972, p. 62.

[38] *Canto 76.*

[39] Williams remarks, "His mind has not budged a hair's breadth . . . he has even entrenched himself more securely."—*The Autobiography of William Carlos Williams* (New York: Random House, 1951), p. 342.

[40] Mary de Rachewiltz, *Discretions,* p. 296.

[41] Interview with Grazia Livi in *Epoca,* March 1963, cited in Harry M. Meacham, *The Caged Panther: Ezra Pound at Saint Elizabeths* (New York: Twayne Publishers, 1967), p. 203.

[42] *Patria Mia,* pp. 64-65.

[43] See Stock, *Poet in Exile,* p. 211. Stock sees Pound, whom he knew well, as very much the product of nineteenth century America.

[44] Letter no. 170, *Selected Letters,* pp. 156-59.

[45] Mary Colum, *Life and the Dream* (New York: Doubleday, 1947), p. 307.

[46] See Michael Reck, *Ezra Pound: A Close-Up,* pp. 117 & 154.

[47] George Steiner, "The Cruellest Months," review of the facsimile edition of T. S. Eliot's *The Waste Land, New Yorker,* April 22, 1972, p. 136.

[48] *Ezra Pound,* ed. Grace Schulman, p. 24.

[49] "The Cruellest Months," 136.

[50] Interview with Donald Hall, reprinted in *Ezra Pound,* ed. Grace Schulman, p. 35.

Pound working on *The Cantos* in the medical compound
of the Detention Training Camp in Pisa, 1945.
(the photo was taken by the U. S. Army and is
reproduced courtesy of Thames & Hudson)

Ezra Pound at Schloss Brunnenberg, 1958
(the photo is by Boris de Rachewiltz and is reproduced courtesy
of Mary de Rachewiltz and the Beinecke Library of Yale University)

T. S. ELIOT'S SEARCH FOR ROOTS

In my beginning is my end. . . .
In my end is my beginning.

There is a satisfaction in following the trajectory of Eliot's career: he is buried in East Coker, the same Somersetshire village from which his ancestors left for America three centuries before his birth. It is tempting to see this poet's progress back to the land of his forefathers as highly deliberate and purposive, yet chance played a part in it too. Though Eliot's life was much more charted and controlled than Pound's, and he was outwardly less battered and baffled by the winds of fortune, Eliot too was subject to unpredictable, irrational forces impinging on him from without and within. Examining the seemingly ineluctable curve of his career, certain episodes stand out as joins or breaks, which made all the difference. Suppose Eliot had, as his parents desired and expected, gone on from distinguished work in graduate school to become a professor of philosophy at Harvard; suppose World War I had not caught him in Germany, hurried him to England, and encouraged him to remain there; suppose he had not contracted the miserable first marriage from which some of his poetry seems to spring, would we then have had his revolutionary poetry, or his enormously influential criticism, or the plays?

Some of the reasons for Eliot's self-exile from the United States are clear; others are obscure. Eliot's life, like his work, *is* obscure and enigmatic. Eliot was a most reticent, evasive, self-effacing, and private man. There could be no greater contrast than that with Joyce, who is shamelessly explicit, self-revealing, confessional even, or with Pound, who can be garrulously self-advertising. Eliot's will stipulated that no biography of him be written—an injunction his widow feels obliged to override.[1] A hushed air of confidentiality pervades even letters of Eliot dealing with the most routine and innocuous matters. Much of the correspondence is inaccessible while Valerie Eliot prepares her late husband's letters for the press, none of it can be quoted without special permission, and some letters cannot be seen until the year 2000 or later, when the people mentioned in them (though one is sure of the utmost discretion of T. S. E. himself) are dead. Eliot frequently destroyed letters or requested that letters from him be destroyed so as to discourage future biographers from invading his privacy. As a result, it may be impossible to determine which of the poet's reasons for self-exile was most important. In the absence of hard evidence, one must speculate. These speculations are informed ones, based on broad and thorough examination, not only of the published work by and about T. S. Eliot, but of unpublished correspondence in various university archives.[2]

Childhood

Exile was in the blood of the Eliot family, who left England for New England and New England for the Middle West. St. Louis, where the poet was born, was a melting-pot city; at the time of his birth, half its population had been born abroad.[3] The Eliot family never considered themselves St. Louisans, nor could Eliot have done, although, back in his birthplace in 1953, he piously declared himself well pleased with having been born in St. Louis.[4] Every summer the Eliots made the long transcontinental train journey to Gloucester, Massachusetts, where the poet's businessman father had bought some land and built a summer house. Thomas Stearns Eliot was educated first in St. Louis —at Smith Academy, the preparatory school for Washington University, which his grandfather founded—then at Milton Academy in Massachusetts. From 1906-14 he was engaged in undergraduate and graduate study at Harvard. Eliot has himself commented on his strong sense of displacement and alienation as a child.

> I want to write an essay about the point of view of an American who wasn't an American, because he was born in the South and went to school in New England as a small boy with a nigger drawl, but who wasn't a southerner in the South because his people were northerners in a border state and looked down on all southerners . . . and who so was never anything anywhere and who therefore

felt himself to be more a Frenchman than an American and more an Englishman than a Frenchman and yet felt that the U.S.A. up to a hundred years ago was a family extension.[5]

Much is packed into this statement: an American who was not an American (see Eliot's "Mélange Adultère de Tout"), and the Eliots' sense of élitism and apartness. That the U.S.A. had ceased to be a "family extension" with the death of the Federalist Party in the early nineteenth century recalls Henry Adams' similar feeling of alienation from democracy and nostalgia for the meritocracy which had recognized his family's right to rule. Eliot's somewhat schizoid childhood, spent shuttling back and forth between the Middle West and New England, made it difficult for him, who had a passion for roots, to feel he belonged in either place. The Boston background sharpened his sense of alienation from St. Louis, and the St. Louisan background his feeling of not being altogether at home even in Boston, the aboriginal preserve of the Eliots. A profound sense of homelessness was the result. Eliot had inherited the deeply conservative, traditional, and élitist attitudes of his forebears, together with their religious sense of social commitment; hence his distaste for the democratic melting pot as exemplified in St. Louis. Yet St. Louis left its mark on this alienated intellectual.

Eliot is preeminently an urban poet, and St. Louis, with its mixed German, French, New England, and Southern population, was one of the most cosmopolitan American cities. Eliot has said that the first twenty-one years of his experience *are* a poet's material.[6] The poet lived in St. Louis for seventeen years; from the ages of eight through seventeen, he divided his time between St. Louis and Boston. Still, Eliot's claim that "Missouri and the Mississippi have made a deeper impression on me than any other part of the world"[7] is not substantiated by his poetry, which is more remarkable for bookishness than for regional flavor. Though Eliot declared a writer cannot be universal without first being local, Eliot himself is rarely local. His poems' cityscapes blend into one another; they are deliberately unparticularized, for the most part, and thus universal. Eliot's images are filtered through the mind and are diffuse, symbolic. One can argue indifferently for St. Louis or Boston as background to Prufrock's mental wanderings. *The Waste Land* is certainly a London poem, but its city is all cities: Jerusalem, Athens, Alexandria, Vienna, and London are rendered indistinguishable from one another. Only in *The Dry Salvages,* which Eliot conceived as a specifically American poem, does he record identifiable images of the "strong brown god" of the Mississippi and of the rocky coast of New England. Yet, as Eliot says of Hawthorne, "the soil of his origin contributed a flavour discriminable after transplantation in his latest fruit."[8] The flavor, in Hawthorne's case and his own, was that of the New England conscience.

Education

Eliot attended Harvard during its Golden Age, when William James, George Santayana, Josiah Royce, Bertrand Russell, George Herbert Palmer, George Lyman Kittredge, George Pierce Baker, and Irving Babbitt were teaching there. Eliot took his A.B. in three years, receiving it in 1909, the same year that his distant cousin, Charles W. Eliot, resigned as President of Harvard (his long tenure of reform had lasted from 1869 to 1909). Like his master, Irving Babbitt, Eliot did not approve of the elective system cousin Charles Eliot had introduced at Harvard on the model of the German universities. The poet thought it good for one's character and necessary for a broad, well founded education to study required subjects. Still, he was the beneficiary of the wealth of scholar-teachers Harvard boasted at the turn of the century, and took courses with James, Santayana, Royce, Russell, Kittredge, Baker, and Babbitt.

Harvard was then pervaded by a cosmopolitan, European atmophere. Eliot's classmate and co-editor of the *Harvard Advocate,* W. G. Tinckom-Fernandez, thought Harvard undergraduates also benefited from rubbing shoulders with graduate students from all over the country. He writes: "the university attracted a host of aspirants for doctors and masters degrees from all over the country, and the college, with its elective system of study, exposed us undergraduates to a variety of stimulating contacts and experiences. I like to account for Eliot's flair for eclectic scholarship . . . by recalling the intellectual excitements in this comparative atmosphere. . . ."[9] The tone of Harvard at this time was European in general and Anglophile in particular. One of the most ardent Anglophiles was Barrett Wendell, who taught Eliot English and American literature. One of the most

Europeanized of his professors was Irving Babbitt, whose course in French literature, together with Eliot's discovery in December 1908 of the French Symbolist poets (through Symons' *The Symbolist Movement in Literature*) was probably the single most important influence on Eliot's education and future vocation. Eliot has often acknowledged the profound influence exerted over him by Irving Babbitt.[10]   Babbitt was a Francophile who imbued his students with his admiration for France and French culture.   Eliot's discovery of the French Symbolist poets, particularly of Baudelaire, Laforgue, and Corbière, was a revelation. Reading them, he found a voice to express what he had to say. Eliot modeled himself on Laforgue in particular; he seemed to regard this expatriate poet, who died the year before he was born, as a sort of poetic avatar. Laforgue, born in Uruguay, had expatriated himself to England. Eliot appears to have imitated his manner of life as well as his style of writing.   Both poets were sober, immaculately dressed dandies whose almost clerical seriousness hid a quizzical humor.   Both were outwardly very correct, in the English manner. In both, a "politic, cautious, and meticulous" manner seems to conceal nervousness and melancholia.

Paris

It was natural that Eliot, given his admiration for the French Symbolist poets should, after taking his baccalaureate, gravitate to Paris in 1910-11.   Babbitt had pointed him in this direction.   Eliot's postgraduate year studying at the Sorbonne and experiencing Europe firsthand for the first time was one of the happiest of his entire life.   It was a period of intellectual ripening for the young American and a time of intense political and cultural activity in France. The Action Française had been founded in 1908, the *Nouvelle Revue Française* in 1909. Eliot had been predisposed by Babbitt to admire Charles Maurras and Julien Benda.   The conservative, traditional, pro-monarchist, anti-democratic climate of Paris appealed to Eliot. (When he described himself in 1927 as classicist in literature, royalist in politics, and Anglo-Catholic in religion, Eliot was repeating a formula by which Maurras had been described in the N.R.F.)[11] Writers, philosophers, and scientists of the stature of Barrès,

Claudel, De Gourmont, Gide, Péguy, Bergson, Durkheim, Janet and Lévy-Bruhl contributed to the intellectual ferment of the capital. Eliot heard Bergson lecture, associated with Alain Fournier and Jacques Rivière, steeped himself in poetry, wrote some, and returned to Harvard, as Conrad Aiken expresses it, "perceptibly Europeanized."[12]

Still following the example of his master, Babbitt, Eliot (who said Babbitt knew more about Eastern thought than anyone in America) enrolled in graduate courses in Sanskrit and Pali and Vedic philosophy. The influence of Indic philosophy on his work is evident, and at one time Eliot even thought of becoming a Buddhist.[13] He was to abandon the study of Indic thought, which left him in "a state of enlightened mystification," because to really penetrate the arcana of Vedic philosophy would have necessitated "forgetting how to think and feel as a European: which . . . I do not wish to do."[14] The period 1911-14 was given over wholly to philosophy, and constituted one of Eliot's "dry" periods for poetry. He appeared to be headed for a distinguished career as a professor of philosophy. Between 1909 and 1911, when he returned to Harvard from France, however, Eliot had written at least half the poems which were to appear in his first volume of verse, *Prufrock & Other Observations.*[15] Poetry must still have been on Eliot's mind as he completed his graduate studies at Harvard. And he must still have been chafing against his native environment after his first taste of Europe.

The obverse of Eliot's love for Europe and desire to cultivate the European mind was his distaste for America. Perhaps he transferred his dream of refuge from the crude hinterland of the Middle West first to Boston and then, finding this merely provincial-colonial after all, to Europe. Paradoxically, receiving his education during Harvard's Golden Era only sharpened his dissatisfaction with the state of the rest of the country. America seemed to Eliot, as it did to Pound, a cultural desert. Boston was the best of it, and Boston Eliot called "uncivilized but refined beyond the point of civilization."[16] While still at Harvard, the resources of New England nonetheless struck Eliot as narrow.[17] Eliot's heart was in Europe even before he went to Paris.[18] Looking back twenty years later at the country he left in 1914, Eliot said: "Younger generations can hardly realize the intellectual desert of England and America during the first decade and more of this century. In the English desert, to be sure, flourished a few tall and handsome cactuses, as well as James and Conrad (for whom the climate, in contrast to their own, was relatively favorable); in America the desert extended, *à perte de vue.* . . . The predominance of Paris was incontestable."[19] What is interesting about this quotation is that Eliot, looking back, sees England as only a little less of a desert than the United States. He is referring to the barrenness of the Anglo-Saxon literary landscape, and he notes among those who cast the longest shadow across the English wasteland transplants from foreign soil, like himself. In a memorial essay on Ezra Pound, Eliot was to remark on the dearth of American poets of any caliber in the period 1900-14: "there was no poet, in either country, who could have been of use to a beginner. . . . The only recourse was to poetry of another age and to poetry of another language."[20] George Santayana, who left Harvard for Europe two years before Eliot, comments how irremediably ugly he found the general tenor of American life. He seems to anticipate Eliot's dictum that modern poetry must be complex, remarking, "The artistic being so foreign, the American artist cannot be unconscious or simple. There are no native 'masters'." Santayana observes that his own generation of Harvard poets all died prematurely, but adds that America would have stifled their talent if they had lived.[21] Eliot's friend and fellow student, Tinckom-Fernandez, says the literary generation of 1910 was driven abroad by the superannuated, jaded, genteel literary environment in America, which was hostile to youthful talent. The motto of the literary pundits of the Genteel Tradition, says Tinckom-Fernandez, might have been "that which is new is not true, and that which is true is not new." He argues that Eliot, had he tried to remain in the United States, would have felt "threatened with spiritual and literary extinction." Just as Pound had been inspired to try his poetic fortune in London by the presence there of Yeats, whom he considered the world's greatest living poet, Eliot was inspired by the example of Pound. (Not that Eliot thought highly of Pound's early verse.) Tinckom-Fernandez says the idea of trying their chances as writers in London first came to Eliot and himself at Harvard when they discussed Pound's journey into exile.[22] Eliot was at first more attracted to Paris than London; his temperament, the pursuit of philosophy, war, and marriage determined he would settle in the latter, not the former. In 1931 Eliot still maintained, "The American intellectual of today has almost no chance of continuous development upon his own

soil. . . . He must be an expatriate: either to languish in a provincial university [these Eliot regarded as oases in the desert] , or
abroad, or, the most complete expatriation of all, in New
York."[23]

In turning to Europe and England, Eliot was also following
the example of Henry James, of which he was surely conscious,
being a great admirer of James. He said of James, a year after
James's death, that he did not suppose it possible for anyone but
an American properly to appreciate James. He envied him for
having been transplanted at so early an age that he had not yet
been thwarted or warped by his native environment. This and
other self-revealing comments imply that Eliot felt, by contrast,
that he had been so warped or thwarted—specifically by puritanism. Thinking of both James and himself, Eliot declared: "It is
the final perfection, the consummation of an American to become, not an Englishman, but a European—something which no
born European . . . can become."[24] What Eliot meant by this
is that a European is born, say, an Englishman, a Frenchman,
or a German and that it is difficult, if not impossible, for him to
achieve the sense of the whole European community that an
American, an outsider, naturally has or may develop. Like
James, Eliot required the traditions, institutions, and sense of
organic interrelatedness of society that James, in his book on
Hawthorne, finds present in Europe and absent from America.
Like James, too, Eliot was drawn first in Europe to Paris, which
has been for so many American writers the magnetic antipole of
the United States. Finally, like James, Eliot settled in London
and became a British subject, although he at first had reservations
about England. His reasons for settling in England were similar
to James's: for an American, Europe is attractive but alien (there
is evidence Eliot found Paris too exotic and stimulating),[25]
whereas England is the bridge between the New and the Old
Worlds and possesses the dual advantages of likeness and difference. England offers the further enormous advantage to a
writer-in-exile of not having to abandon his own language—although during his year in Paris in 1910-11, Eliot seriously considered doing so and writing in French.[26]

Anyone who goes into exile voluntarily may be presumed to
have both positive and negative reasons for doing so. Strongest
of positive reasons is the desire for a new start, and of negative
reasons, the feeling of having reached the end of something and
of needing to escape conditions that are thwarting or stultifying.

Paradoxically, Eliot's new start was to be a beginning over again on the ground his ancestors had left and the embracement of the religion and nationality they had rejected. Eliot exchanged his old life in the New World for a new life in the Old World. For he had never felt at home at home. The America he loved was a thing of the past when he was born. Eliot viewed the election of Andrew Jackson in 1828 as the beginning of the end of the American Republic run by meritocracy, and as leading to the Civil War, a catastrophe from which the United States has never recovered.[27] (This is in line with Roy Nichols' theory in *The Disruption of American Democracy* that the Civil War was brought on by the excesses of mass politics.) Eliot, like Henry Adams, felt himself one of a displaced élite, an old ruling class superseded by parvenu democracy. Pound's sensibility was different, yet he too indulged in reactionary nostalgia for the early days of the Republic—though his aristocratic hero, Jefferson, was looked at askance by Eliot, the Hamiltonian Federalist. Eliot was as much in love with the past as Pound was; such a love of the past could be satisfied only by and in Europe. Both Pound and Eliot were exiles in time as well as space. Eliot's sense of the past is strong and deep—powerful as he said only an American's sense of the past could be.[28] Presumably because Americans have been severed from their roots and transplanted, they may have a preternaturally keen, objective sense of their past origins. Eliot had a lifelong obsession with the resurrection of the past, with bringing the dead to life again and making them speak.

Europe

Eliot's immediate means of leaving America for Europe was a Sheldon Fellowship from Harvard enabling him to travel and study for his dissertation abroad during the year 1914-15. He went first neither to London nor Paris but to the University of Marburg. Germany was recommended for the study of Idealist philosophy. In 1913 Eliot had read F. H. Bradley and projected a thesis comparing Bradley's theory of knowledge with Meinong's *Gegenstandstheorie*. At this time Eliot intended going into permanent exile no more than Pound had in 1908—indeed less. Eliot's sensibility, attitudes, education, and ambitions drew him to Europe; war and marriage combined to keep him away from home.

Part of the summer of 1914 Eliot spent traveling around Europe; he had been in Germany only two weeks when war broke out. War hurried Eliot to England and Merton College, Oxford, where he had already arranged to study Aristotle under Harold Joachim, starting in the autumn term. War was not yet, therefore, responsible for changing the course of his life so much as for expediting it. Correspondence shows Eliot disliked Germany and felt bored and isolated there. He found the Germans uncivilized but could not condemn them outright as belligerents. He pointed out they were fighting for their lives.[29] Eliot's attitude to war was extraordinarily complex: essentially he believed that no one ever knows enough about any war to assign blame correctly or to distinguish just from unjust motives for resorting to violence. With a profound sense of the evil and violence of the times, Eliot thought one might be personally justified in participating in war, even while fighting on the "wrong" side. He dismayed his old teacher, Bertrand Russell, by not being a pacifist.[30] Eliot was rejected as a combatant because of congenital hernia and tachycardia. A year after the United States entered World War I, he was trying to find a position in U. S. Naval or Army Intelligence, and was still tied up in red tape when the armistice came. Eliot does not appear to have shared Henry James's horror of war. He accepted it fatalistically. Asked by Stephen Spender in 1930 what he foresaw as the future of western civilization, Eliot responded darkly, "Internecine fighting. . . . People killing one another in the streets."[31]

Oxford

Eliot's first impressions of England, which he reached at the end of August 1914, were definitely unfavorable. The University of Oxford, bereft by conscription of most of its students, struck him as a morgue. To Aiken he wrote, "Oxford is very pretty, but I don't like to be dead."[32] In addition, Eliot was beginning to find the study of philosophy deadening.[33] He deplored English food, weather, and the stultifying conversation of the dons and their wives. Indeed, he thought he would never get to like England. One of Eliot's biographers, T. S. Matthews, has asked, "If he did not like the country or the people or even the food they ate, what was it that drew Eliot so powerfully to England, estranging him from his native land and straining the ties that bound him to his family?"[34]

Eliot's own sensibility and thirst for knowledge drew him to the continent and then to England. His temperament was ideally suited to England, which grew on him as he on her. Brand Blanshard, who knew Eliot at Oxford, has declared that "by temperament he was a born Englishman . . . he was reserved, shy, economical of speech, rather frostily formal of manner. . . . He was not by temperament or conviction a democrat."[35] Eliot studied at Oxford from October 1914 to July 1915. Bradley taught at Oxford, but Eliot never met him, for Bradley was ill and saw few students.

Some time in the spring of 1915, T. S. Eliot met Vivienne Haigh-Wood, whom he married on June 26, 1915 without the knowledge of either his or her parents. The Haigh-Woods subsequently blessed the marriage, but Eliot's parents were dismayed by it. Eliot was summoned home that summer to give an account of himself; his wife did not accompany him for fear of submarines. Although he continued his allowance to him on condition that he finish his doctoral thesis, Eliot's father was never reconciled to his son's marriage or his later abandonment of philosophy for poetry. By this marriage, which kept him in England, Eliot was disappointing his parents' hopes of a brilliant career for him teaching philosophy at Harvard. When Henry Ware Eliot, Sr. died in 1919, Thomas Stearns was the only one of his children to whom he left no outright bequest. The memory of the last meeting with his father in 1915 and of the failure of reconciliation was to haunt Eliot.[36]

Marriage

> The awful daring of a moment's surrender
> Which an age of prudence can never retract.

These lines, like so many in Eliot's ostensibly impersonal poetry, are charged with deep personal meaning. They could well refer to his unfortunate first marriage. Biographers and critics have speculated whether the poet may have been somehow constrained or compromised into an ill-considered alliance with a

woman who was physically sickly, mentally unstable, and socially his inferior. One can only speculate too whether exile and the
marriage which set the seal on it were not both a rebellion
against smothering family ties. When Eliot met her, Vivienne
Haigh-Wood was a dark, pretty, vivacious, febrile girl with a
talent for ballet and ballroom dancing. In the words of Bertrand
Russell, who knew the couple well, having given them a room in
his London flat, Vivienne was "light, a little vulgar, adventurous,
full of life . . . I should have thought her an actress. He is exquisite and listless; she said she married him in order to stimulate
him, but finds she can't do it. Obviously he married to be stimu-
lated. . . . He is ashamed of his marriage, and very grateful if
one is kind to her."[37] Eliot became for Russell a sort of adopted
son. Because Russell was a notorious womanizer, and because he
acceded to Tom's request to look after Vivienne while he was
working on his dissertation—even, at her husband's urging, taking
Vivienne for a short vacation to Torquay in January 1916—the
Russell-Eliot relationship has been seen as a *ménage-à-trois* and
Russell has been accused of adultery with Vivienne.[38]
    Like so much else in his life, Eliot kept his marriage private.
He was extremely secretive about this, as about most aspects
of his life. Again, his motives for marrying Vivienne are a matter
of speculation. No doubt at the time he met her Eliot felt he
needed someone just like her to enliven his existence. He was
passive and listless, suffered from what he called abulia or willess-
ness,[39] and especially after a year at Oxford, wanted to be gal-
vanized into life. Instead, his wife proved to be a constant drain
on his social life, his finances, and what nervous energy he had.
She suffered from colds, bronchitis, influenza, colitis, palpita-
tions, and insomnia. She was under constant, costly supervision
by specialists and forever taking cures. She turned Eliot, a hypo-
chondriac himself, into a male nurse. Gradually she was dropped
from his social invitations. Eliot's sexual inexperience, his kind-
ness, his invalidism, and his masochism alike drew him to
Vivienne.[40] Russell, whom Eliot called a "great psychologist"
and whose diagnosis of his marital problems he finally came to
accept, said of the young couple: "I endeavoured to help them
in their troubles until I discovered that their troubles were what
they really enjoyed."[41] Russell perceived in Vivienne a Dos-
toievskian cruelty towards her husand which struggled for a
while against his saintly patience with her. Another friend, who
has recorded a vivid vignette of the Eliots happy dancing to-

gether, observes of Eliot that "he loved not only his own, but the pain of others."[42]   From the first, Eliot regarded marriage as a test or ordeal of one's whole character for life, a test which he accepted with a curious mixture of puritan zeal and martyred resignation.[43]   The "awful daring," the haste, and the impulsive recklessness with which he entered into this marriage were totally at odds with Eliot's normally cautious and prudent manner. Though the marriage was so self-destructive as to seem almost suicidal, it obviously satisfied some psychological need of Eliot's. The termination of his philosophical studies at Oxford may have seemed to Eliot a dead end, in the literal sense; Vivienne was the lifeline he grasped at desperately to give himself a new direction and new responsibilities and to prevent himself having to return home to the old ones. But what had been intended as an anchor became a millstone. Perhaps guilt at rebelling against an overprotective mother led to a masochistic marriage to an overdependent girl who eventually became an unloved burden.   Above all, Vivienne was to be responsible for keeping her husband in England. Those who see Eliot as a careerist, carefully making his way by always associating with the right people and shunning the wrong sort, should consider the handicap he gave himself in marrying such a wife. He was forever having to cater to her every whim and apologize for her. It is interesting that both Eliot's marriages—although the one he contracted in his sixties was as happy as the one he made in his twenties was miserable—were to women of a lower social class than his (i.e. middle class, while Eliot was upper middle class). No social climber would have married Vivienne Haigh-Wood.

The Conquest of London

Eliot's conquest of the London literary world began against tremendous odds in 1915, which was for him a crucial year. This was the year in which Eliot abandoned philosophy for poetry, and in which he married and decided to remain in England. Richard Ellmann affirms that Eliot "was helped to all three decisions by Ezra Pound. . . . He encouraged Eliot to marry and settle, and he read the poems that no one had been willing to publish," and, further, he got them published.[44] Eliot's meeting with Pound took place in Pound's diminutive Kensington apart-

ment on September 22, 1914, prior to Eliot's period of study at
Oxford. Eliot recalled making a good impression at this interview, and Pound hailed his young compatriot as the only poet
who has "actually trained himself *and* modernized himself *on
his own.*"[45]   Pound certainly encouraged and helped Eliot to
make poetry his vocation. Pound was married to an Englishwoman, and Valerie Eliot says he encouraged Eliot to marry
Vivienne Haigh-Wood as a means of keeping Eliot for English
letters.[46]

Eliot's correspondence indicates that the decision to abandon philosophy coincided with the decision to marry and settle
in England. Like Pound when he first arrived there, Eliot felt
London was the best place to be if one wished to make one's
mark on the literary world.[47]   As a result of war, Paris had become impossible. Letters home show the war raised obstacles to
a young poet's making his way in the London literary world
too.[48]   Literature took a backseat to jingo journalism and propaganda; paper was scarce; literary jobs and outlets were curtailed.
War made it twice as difficult for Eliot; so, of course, did his marriage. It is twice as hard to support two as one, and his wife,
utterly dependent, was always ill and in need of medical care.
Eliot's own health broke down as a result of chronic overwork
and fatigue.

Valerie Eliot's facsimile edition of *The Waste Land* has been
a revelation, for it revealed for the first time the enormous obstacles Eliot the man encountered, and over which Eliot the poet-
critic triumphed. There were his years of schoolmastering in
High Wycombe and Hampstead at £140 and £160, respectively,
with evening extension lectures to prepare and deliver and
numerous book reviews and articles to write. Eliot disliked
teaching and would later turn down appointments at the most
prestigious universities because teaching entailed a projection of
personality which he found exhausting.[49]   Lecturing too he
found fatiguing, but he preferred it to reading his own poetry,
which was too much like undressing in public![50]   Eliot enjoyed
critical writing and reviewing but was compelled to do it early in
the morning before leaving for work, late in the evening after
returning from his daily grind, or over weekends. He feared too
much reviewing would drown out his own creative powers. Writing poetry itself was like being visited and possessed by some ter-
rifying demonic force, whose visitations one could neither insure
nor prevent, hasten nor forestall, but must wait for and suffer

patiently. Poetry was possession, despite Eliot's critical pronouncements which decry romantic inspiration and uphold instead deliberate, painstaking craftmanship. Leonard Unger sums up well the conflict between Eliot's critical theory of poetry and his poetry in practice. As Unger says, "His criticism urged a program of the classical, the traditional, and the impersonal, while he was producing a poetry which is poignantly romantic, strikingly modernist, and intensely personal."[51]

In 1917, through his in-laws, Eliot obtained a position in the Colonial and Foreign Department of Lloyds Bank. He worked there for eight years, putting in long hours and frequently a six-day week, but preferring it to teaching. Banking provided a complete break with literary activities, so he was fresher when he returned to them. (There is a parallel with Wallace Stevens, who also found the routine business of settling insurance claims somehow liberating.) Eliot's many languages were invaluable to his job, and he was prized by his employers, eventually rising to a salary of £600.

Meanwhile, Pound was helping his new protégé in the literary world. He introduced Eliot to Harriet Shaw Weaver, co-editor of *The Egoist,* and when Richard Aldington resigned the assistant editorship of that journal to go into the army, Eliot replaced him. Part of Eliot's small salary was secretly contributed by Pound. Pound was responsible for getting Eliot's first volume of poems, *Prufrock & Other Observations,* published in 1917 by The Egoist Press; he footed part of the printing bill himself. Pound was also instrumental, through John Quinn, in getting Eliot's *Poems* and first volume of criticism published in America. Pound later conceived the Bel Esprit scheme, whereby some thirty patrons of the arts were secretly to subscribe £10 per year for an indefinite period to release Eliot from his bank work so he might devote his full time and energy to his writing. News of this scheme leaked to its prospective beneficiary and, Eliot finding it distasteful and bordering on charity, it was dropped. Pound was of considerable assistance to Eliot in getting him started during his first and most difficult years in London. Pound himself had a hard time making a living by his pen during, and particularly after, the war, but Donald Gallup points out that, thanks to his wife's settlement, Pound at first suffered less financial hardship than Eliot.[52] By the time Pound had antagonized most of London's editors, lost his own editorial posts and publishing outlets, and decamped for Paris, Eliot was in a position to help Pound. He did so by securing for him the position of Paris correspondent for *The Dial.* Eliot and Pound were, in a sense, to change places, for although Pound had not been, as Eliot was to become, London's literary dictator, he had been London's most enterprising and indefatigable literary entrepreneur and practitioner.

Despite a life full of anxiety, illness, overwork, and exhaustion, Eliot was making his way. Pound had "boomed" him and provided him with useful literary contacts; he made many more for himself. Through Bertrand Russell he became a member of the circle of talent surrounding Lady Ottoline Morrell at Garsington. Eliot's relations with Bloomsbury were outwardly cordial; his letters show that he held himself aloof from several members of the Bloomsbury Group, though his friendship with the Woolfs was quite close and lasting. Leonard and Virginia Woolf published Eliot's *Poems 1919* under their Hogarth Press imprint. Eliot's first collection of critical essays, *The Sacred Wood,* published in 1920, announced the advent of an important new critic and gave Eliot a critical following. In 1919 he was introduced to Bruce Richmond, editor of the *TLS,* and began writing editorials for that prestigious paper. John Middleton Murray, for whom Eliot wrote a number of articles, offered him the assistant editorship of *The Athenaeum,* which Eliot declined. Nevertheless, after *The Egoist* was discontinued, Eliot was casting about for a journal he could edit. This was some time in materializing, but by the summer of 1921 Eliot knew he had possession of a new organ, *The Criterion,* which he intended using as a vehicle to express "the keenest sensibility and the clearest thought" of the time, not only in literature, but in philosophy, sociology, economics, politics, and religion.[53]

The Criterion was, in its early years, financed by Lady Rothermere. Eliot was given a completely free hand as editor, but he never earned a penny for all his labor in running it, because Lloyd's had a rule that its employees must earn no outside income. In 1922, when *The Criterion* began, Eliot felt that his own career depended on the success or failure of the journal; he wrote Aldington that he staked his future on the journal's and that, if it should fail, he would lose his usefulness and prestige in the field of English letters, and would have to "retire to obscurity and Paris like Ezra."[54] In fact, *The Criterion* was a most prestigious journal, which lasted sixteen years, from October 1922 to January 1939. Though it never had a wide readership, it fulfilled Eliot's ambitions by publishing much of the finest and most wide-ranging international criticism, fiction, and poetry, particularly during the twenties. In 1926, Faber & Gwyer, the publishing firm Eliot had joined after his resignation from the bank, took over the journal from Lady Rothermere, who withdrew her sponsorship when she found *The Criterion* insufficiently chic for her taste. In the thirties, after its editor's conversion, *The Criterion* adopted a more and more religious tone and outlook, becoming, as Pound put it, more and more heavily disguised as Westminster Abbey and a fitting spokesman for "the mortician's parlour which is England."[55]

Between 1917 and 1921 Eliot carried out, in the time he could spare from earning a living, "what must be the most arduous . . . concentrated critical labor of which detailed record exists . . . a rethinking of the traditional heritage of English letters."[56] Eliot's critical method was, like his method of writing poetry, a combination of passive submission and active deliberation, designed to fuse objectivity with subjectivity. What the American poet-critic brought to London that revolutionized English criticism was a scholarship so rigorous it insisted on reading all of an author's work, however much that might be, before presuming to criticize it. To Stephen Spender Eliot confided his strenuous procedure of soaking up *all* a writer's work before gathering himself to pronounce upon it: "you have to give yourself up, and then recover yourself, and the third moment is having something to say, before you have wholly forgotten both surrender and recovery. Of course the self recovered is never the same as the self before it was given."[57]   Once again, characteristically, Eliot's emphasis is on submission and surrender of the self to something other.

The first issue of *The Criterion* contained both Eliot's *The Waste Land* and Valéry Larbaud's exposition of Joyce's *Ulysses*. "Prufrock" had made Eliot known to the cognoscenti of the English-speaking literary world; *The Waste Land* put him on the world's literary map. But until Valerie Eliot published the lost manuscript of *The Waste Land* readers had no notion of the labor, on Pound's as well as Eliot's part, which went into the making of that poem, and until one read his widow's introduction to the facsimile edition of the poem, one had little idea of the agony Eliot was going through when he composed it. 1921 was another crucial year for the poet. *The Waste Land* was composed while he was undergoing a nervous breakdown due to

worry, overwork, and exhaustion.   During the summer, Eliot
had been visited by his mother, sister, and brother.   It was the
first time his mother had met his bride or seen her son since the
chilly family reunion six years earlier.   Tom and Vivienne vacated
their flat at 9 Clarence Gate Gardens so that the family from
America could occupy it.   Against doctor's orders, Vivienne
stayed in town to meet her in-laws.   Eliot must have been extremely edgy and uneasy.[58]   When his relatives left and the ten-
sion eased, Eliot suffered a decline.   In the fall, a nervous special-
ist Eliot consulted ordered him to take three months off and not
to write at all.   Lloyds gave him a paid leave of absence.   Eliot
went first to Margate with Vivienne—"On Margate Sands./I can
cannect/Nothing with nothing"—then to Lausanne—"By the
waters of Leman I sat down and wept. . . ."   In Switzerland the
poet was under the care of Dr. Roger Vittoz, Lady Ottoline
Morrell's physician, for a month.   In the sanatorium the larger
breakdown of Europe was reflected and echoed in the voices of
the other patients which are recorded in *The Waste Land*.   By
January 1922 Eliot had delivered to Pound in Paris the typescript
of the long poem he had been ruminating for over two years.[59]
Pound's editing of the poem has and will be matter of controversy for years.   Perhaps Eliot's breakdown and his debilitated
state help explain his submissiveness in accepting Pound's ex-
cisions and emendations.   To a few readers it may even seem he
was abdicating an author's responsibility for his own work,
exiling himself from it, so to speak.

    With the almost simultaneous publication of *The Waste
Land* in *The Criterion* for October and *The Dial* in America for
November 1922, and his winning of The Dial Prize of $2,000,
Eliot's troubles were far from over.   Three months after his return from Switzerland, Aldington told Pound that Eliot was
going to pieces again.[60]   Both Eliots continued to suffer from ill
health.   In the summer of 1922, Eliot's father-in-law financed a
two week vacation for him in Northern Italy; Eliot met Pound
again in Verona.   Their letters show that 1923 was a particularly
bad year for the Eliots.   After devoting nearly all his spare time
to *The Criterion* for eighteen months, without remuneration,
Eliot found himself with neither time nor energy to give to his
own writing or even to mundane chores that demanded his attention.   In March 1923 he wrote John Quinn, "I am worn out, I
cannot go on."[61]   He and his wife were both ill; Vivienne was, as
her husband thought, on a couple of occasions at the point of

death. She spent considerable time convalescing in their country cottage at Fishbourne.

Against such odds, Eliot had gradually made a place for himself in England. London had grown on him, as he had on his future compatriots. London discloses her charms in leisurely fashion, and the English are slow to warm to outsiders. Eliot enjoyed the anonymity of life in this great metropolis. Though he had few intimate friends, he had a wide circle of influential acquaintance and he knew, unlike Pound, how to ingratiate himself. Pound's nickname for Eliot, Old Possum, was well chosen: it suggests his inveterate caution and discretion. He rarely committed himself and, when cornered, could "play dead," as it were. Nothing could have contrasted more sharply than these two poets' social styles. Ez's aggressive, hectoring manner antagonized the English, while Possum's quiet good manners commended him to them. To most people he was not noticeably American, but seemed like one of their own. There were exceptions. Lady Ottoline Morrell, meeting Eliot for the first time at Garsington, where he was obviously on his best manners, found him "dull, dull, dull. He never moves his lips but speaks in an even and monotonous voice, and I felt him monotonous without and within. . . . He is obviously very ignorant of England and imagines that it is essential to be highly polite and conventional and decorous, and meticulous." Looking back to this first encounter, which seems to have taken place in 1915, however, Lady Ottoline acknowledges "how odd it was . . . how very foreign Eliot seemed to me then."[62] Sir Herbert Read's recollections of Eliot are more typical. "I was never conscious that he was in any way less English than myself. From the first he fitted naturally into English clothes and English clubs, into English habits generally." Read adds, "If anything gave him away it was an Englishness which was a shade too correct to be natural."[63] Eliot was to become more English than the English. Just as the English artistocracy was too eccentric for his taste, Bloomsbury was too unconventional and bohemian.

In entrenching himself in England, Eliot was also making the best of a bad job. Whenever he could, he would escape to Europe for a brief vacation, as he did in the summer of 1919 with Pound, and in the summer of 1920 with Wyndham Lewis. Eliot was not, however, a born traveler or tourist like Pound and Joyce. All his life he was apprehensive about traveling, except when he could do so by boat. Though he enjoyed brief spells on the continent, Eliot did not wish to live in Europe. Valerie Eliot says that after 1915 he never considered leaving London.[64] He had put down roots and achieved too much in England to abandon it. When others applied to him for advice as to whether they should settle abroad, Eliot advised them against it.[65] He maintained London was the best place for an artist to follow his vocation. Pound unequivocally condemned postwar London's literary scene; Eliot called it "the high summer of literary journalism."[66] Paris, which had exerted such a magnetic attraction on him ten years before, by the twenties seemed too stimulating. Eliot seems to have been intensely aware and chary of the intellectual competition in that capital, and to have disapproved of the dissipation of the American expatriate colony there. Writing to an American expatriate in 1921, Eliot remarked: "If I came to live in Paris the first thing to do would be to cut myself off from it, and not depend upon it." In the same letter, he admires Joyce (then in Paris) for being "independent of outside stimulus, and . . . therefore likely to go on producing first rate work until he dies."[67]

Though his marriage was still sufficient pretext to avoid returning to his motherland, Eliot's wife was now keen that her husband leave England for Europe. In 1922, after returning to London from the sanatorium in Paris where she stayed while Eliot was in Dr. Vittoz's sanatorium in Lausanne, Vivienne wrote Richard Aldington that, when she first met Tom Eliot, she had fought to keep him in England and prevent him returning to America, because she knew their marriage depended on his remaining in England. After the war, however, Vivienne fell completely out of love with England and hoped her husband would follow Ezra Pound's example and leave.[68] His marriage had kept Eliot in England six years previously; it continued to do so. It is most unlikely he would have wanted or been able to start anew elsewhere still carrying the burden imposed on him by his first wife. That Eliot did not wish, despite Pound's urgings, to follow him to Paris is apparent from the letter he wrote Aldington at about this time, in which he equates failure with retiring "to obscurity or Paris like Ezra." Eliot was no quitter. Perseverance was one of his strongest qualities. The Eliot family motto was *Tace et fac*—do and be silent—a motto he seems to have taken to heart. He was doing too well publicly, although his private life was a mess, to leave the field. Having put down roots, he would not tear them up.

1925 was a year of religious crisis, reflected in "The Hollow Men," and followed by a long period of poetic aridity. It was a discouraging year in most respects, but it was the year in which Eliot left Lloyd's, found a job with the publishing firm of Faber & Gwyer (later Faber & Faber), and finally turned the corner financially.[69] From this time on, however ill his wife was, Eliot was better able to provide for her. In 1927 the religious crisis was resolved when Eliot became an Anglo-Catholic. It was less a conversion than a coming home to the church his forefathers had left in the seventeenth century. Eliot had always felt the need of a faith and allegiance to an outside, suprapersonal force. In 1927 he also became a British subject.

Eliot's religious conversion coincided with a drought of poetic inspiration, which was heralded by "The Hollow Men" and broken by *Ash Wednesday*. *Ash Wednesday*, lacking the fusion of thought and image of the early poems and only struggling towards the lucidity with which Eliot invests the deepest mysteries in the *Four Quartets*, is obviously a poem expressing resignation after the agonies attendant on the breakup of his first marriage. When Eliot decided to accept the invitation to give the Charles Eliot Norton lectures at Harvard in 1932-33, returning home for the first time for seventeen years, he also chose this occasion to abandon Vivienne. From the United States in February 1933 he sent her a deed of separation drawn up by his solicitor. He had arranged to support Vivienne for the rest of her life, but to live with her no longer. Eliot made this decision and acted on it alone, without consulting his wife. Apparently, he could not face a direct confrontation; this was the way he believed the break had to be made. Vivienne was shocked. On his return to England, she pursued her husband pathetically but in vain.

It it interesting that, just as his marriage had been a prime reason for Eliot's prolonging his exile in England, his return to his native land coincided with the end of this marriage. Herbert Howarth has remarked that only in Eliot's later work does he use the poetic material stored up since his Missouri-Massachusetts childhood. "In the work written during the long, unbroken 1914-32 absence from his homeland he was unable to use it. His face was averted" through dislike and guilt.[70] His letters from America show that Eliot was still highly critical of his homeland, and felt scarcely more at home there than he had in his youth, but that he enjoyed being back where he had begun, among family and friends who had been fond of him before "the malady of poetry declared itself."[71] Like Harry in *The Family Reunion*, an obliquely autobiographical play, Eliot had felt the "instinct to return to the point of departure."[72] His settlement in England had been motivated by the same instinct, in a sense. In 1934 Eliot returned to America, this time to the South, where he gave the Page-Barbour lectures at the University of Virginia. He made many subsequent visits to the United States during the latter half of his life, including those to the Institute of Advanced Studies in Princeton in 1948, to the University of Chicago in 1950, and to the University of Minnesota in 1956. But Eliot disliked the publicity which pursued him in his country of origin and grew homesick for London, never wanting to spend more than a year away from England, particularly during the war.[73]

Still, he seems to have liked shuttling back and forth between England and America, having a foot in each country. "It is a privilege to live . . . in two cultures, and I am grateful for it. Each is more interesting because of the contrast with the other. I believe I have the best of both possible worlds," he said.[74]

Eliot's life from the thirties through the fifties seemed like the gradual extinction of personality he advocates for the poet in "Tradition and the Individual Talent." Established as the most influential literary critic of the English-speaking world, powerful too in publishing circles, Eliot's private life became more and more religious, self-abnegating, and self-effacing. When he returned to England after his year at Harvard, he did not return to London (Vivienne still occupied the Eliot's apartment), but took refuge with his American colleague at Faber & Faber, Frank Morley, on his farm in Surrey.[75] For twenty-five years Eliot served as a church-warden at St. Stephen's, his church in Gloucester Road, Kensington. For six years after the breakup of his marriage in 1933, he lived as a paying guest with his vicar, the Reverend Cheetham. It was through working for the church that Eliot became a dramatist. *The Rock* was written for a London church-building fund and resulted in an invitation to write a play for the Canterbury Festival in 1935—*Murder in the Cathedral*. During the war, Eliot spent four days a week in London, working, firewatching, and sleeping at his publishing office, and three days with his friends, the Mirrlees, in Surrey. For nine years in the late forties and fifties he lived with John Hayward, a scholar confined to a wheelchair by muscular dystrophy. Eliot had first met Hayward as an undergraduate at Cambridge, when Eliot gave the Clark Lectures there in 1926. Having rid himself of an invalid wife whom he nursed unavailingly for seventeen years, Eliot took on the care of another invalid. The Hayward ménage was quite convivial, but Eliot's room in the apartment in Cheyne Walk (below one Henry James had once occupied) was monastic in its austerity. Apparently Eliot seriously thought of retiring to a monastery in his old age. He was saved from this by his last, happy marriage.

On January 10, 1957, the poet married Valerie Fletcher, who had been his secretary at Faber & Faber for eight years. Though separated from his first wife, Eliot still considered himself religiously bound to her while she lived. Vivienne died in a mental asylum in January 1947. Eliot's second marriage, like his conversion, baptism, and confirmation, took place secretly. (Just as Vivienne had been given no advance warning that her husband was leaving her, so Eliot did not confide in John Hayward until his second marriage was almost a *fait accompli.* This caused an estrangement between the two men.)[76] Eliot married Valerie Fletcher at St. Barnabas' Church, Kensington, which he was later delighted to discover was the same church in which Jules Laforgue took Leah Lee to wife. The wedding breakfast took place in Pound's old apartment at 10 Church Walk. Eliot said his last years were his happiest, happy beyond anything he felt he could have deserved. One wonders whether, if Eliot had known in his first marriage the happiness, stability, mental health, and serenity he found in his second, he would have written the poetry and the criticism which set the tone and standards for an age. He was born to be a writer, but the tone of his work, had his life been happier, would likely have been different.

In his old age Eliot was frequently ill. In 1950 he suffered a mild heart attack. In the sixties he developed emphysema and, no longer able to withstand the cold and fog of English winters, wintered abroad, in Cape Town with the Fabers or with Valerie in the Caribbean. Looking back over his life, he regarded it as a Dostoevsky novel written by J. Middleton Murry.[77] His suffering and horror before the facts of life ("Birth and copulation and death. That's all"—and Eliot often makes birth and death seem virtually indistinguishable) had been overlaid but not concealed by decorum.

In 1937 Eliot had visited the home of his ancestors, East Coker, for the first time. Though he had earned his place and has a plaque in Poet's Corner, Westminster Abbey, Eliot is buried in East Coker. "Home is where one starts from. . . . In my end is my beginning." Eliot said we cannot fully understand anyone or grasp the totality of his being until he is dead.[78]   Only then, if then, can we perceive a man's entelechy, recognize what he was, where he has been, and what he was tending toward all his life. Eliot began his life as an alienated American and ended it an assimilated Englishman.   He acknowledged in himself character-istics of both nationalities.   Nevertheless, he regarded himself as an American poet, saying that his poetry would not be "what it is if I'd been born in England, and it wouldn't be what it is if I'd stayed in America . . . in its sources, in its emotional springs, it comes from America."[79]   Apart from the pervasive presence of the modern city, a handful of New England seascapes, and some images of the English countryside, Eliot's two environments are only dimly mirrored in his work.   The motive springs of Eliot's art are internal; his landscapes are inscapes suffused by his own peculiar sensibility.

Eliot left America because he never felt at home there: democracy, egalitarianism, centralized government, mass civiliza-tion, sheer size, emphasis on the present, ignorance of and lack of interest in the past, the dearth of tradition and culture—all these and other aspects of American life drove him to Europe. Eliot remained in England because it suited his formal, conserva-tive, traditional, and élitist temperament.   He felt at home in England; it was the best place for him to put down roots.   He could live in England and continue to avail himself of the rich resources of his mother tongue.   He saw England as the bridge between the Old World and the New, and himself as a mediator between old and new, past and present.   Eliot influenced his chosen environment much more than either Pound or Joyce, for Joyce in Europe was forever transfixed, looking back at Dublin, and Pound remained deracinated all his life.   Eliot dominated English literary life for three decades or more.   English poetry and criticism of the modern period, from 1910 through 1940, bear the unmistakable imprint of this exile who mediated be-tween two worlds.

NOTES

[1] In an interview with Timothy Wilson in *The Observer,* February 20, 1972, p. 21, Valerie Eliot explained the best defense against innuendoes and misconceptions about Eliot in recent reviews and unofficial biographies would be an authoritative life. The definitive biography, however, must await Mrs. Eliot's publication of her late husband's letters. In correspondence, she says the first volume of Eliot's letters should appear in 1984 and that, although no official biographer has yet been appointed, she has someone in mind. Mrs. Eliot describes the necessary qualifications for a biographer in *The Observer* interview cited above.

[2] For permission to examine unpublished correspondence of Eliot, I wish to express my thanks to Mrs. Valerie Eliot and the following libraries: the Houghton Library of Harvard University; Princeton University Library; Cornell University Library; Lockwood Memorial Library of the State University of New York at Buffalo, and the Humanities Research Center of the University of Texas at Austin.

[3] Thomas Stanley Matthews, *Great Tom* (New York: Harper & Row, 1973), p. 2.

[4] "American Literature and the American Language," *To Criticize the Critic* (London: Faber & Faber, 1965), p. 45.

[5] Sir Herbert Read, "T. S. E. - A Memoir," in Allen Tate, ed., *The Sewanee Review,* Eliot Memorial Issue, 74 (January-March 1966), 35.

[6] "Turgenev," *The Egoist,* 4 (December 1971), 167.

[7] Eliot's Preface to Edgar A. Mowrer's *This American World* cited by Russell Kirk, *Eliot & His Age: T. S. Eliot's Moral Imagination in the Twentieth Century* (New York: Random House, 1971), p. 25.

[8] "The Hawthorne Aspect," *The Little Review,* 5 (August 1918), 47-48.

[9] *Harvard Advocate,* Special Eliot Number, 125 (December 1938), 6.

[10] See "The Humanism of Irving Babbitt," "Second Thoughts About Humanism," and Eliot's essay in Frederick Manchester & Odell Shepard, eds., *Irving Babbitt: Man & Teacher* (New York: G. P. Putnams Sons, 1941).

[11] See Matthews, *Great Tom,* p. 108.

[12] "King Bolo & Others," in Richard March & Tambimuttu, eds., *T. S. Eliot: A Symposium* (Chicago: Henry Regnery Company, 1949), p. 21.

[13] Stephen Spender, "Remembering Eliot," in Allen Tate, ed., *The Sewanee Review,* 74 (January-March 1966), 60.

[14] Matthews, p. 34; Herbert Howarth, *Some Figures Behind T. S. Eliot* (Boston, Mass.: Houghton Mifflin Company, 1964), p. 206.

[15] Donald Gallup, *T. S. Eliot & Ezra Pound: Collaborators in Letters*

(New Haven: Wenning & Stonehill, Inc., 1970), p. 4.

[16]"The Hawthorne Aspect," *The Little Review*, 5 (August 1918), 49.

[17]"Gentlemen & Seamen," review in *Harvard Advocate*, 87 (May 25, 1909), 15-16.

[18]See Eliot's review of Van Wyck Brooks's *The Wine of the Puritans* in *Harvard Advocate*, 87 (May 7, 1909), 80. Eliot refers to himself indirectly in this review as one of "divided allegiance," whose heart is in Europe. This book obviously affected him profoundly.

[19]"Commentary," *Criterion*, 13 (April 1934), 451.

[20]"Ezra Pound," *Poetry*, 68 (September 1946), 326.

[21]"Marginal Notes on Civilization in the United States," *Dial*, 72 (June 1922), 560, 563-64.

[22]*Harvard Advocate*, 125 (December 1938), 7-8, 47.

[23]"Commentary," *Criterion*, 10 (January 1931), 307-14. Eliot was reviewing *I'll Take My Stand*. Interestingly, this was written a year before Eliot had returned to the United States for the first time in seventeen years. Perhaps his visit changed his mind. Presumably he did not include Harvard among "provincial universities." Although he is cosmopolitan, Eliot did not unequivocally approve of cosmopolitanism; his dislike of New York is due to its being the fiercest melting pot of all.

[24]"In Memory of Henry James," *The Egoist*, 5 (January 1918), 1-2.

[25]In a letter to Robert McAlmon dated May 2, 1921, Eliot writes: "The chief danger about Paris is that it is such a strong stimulus." Cited in Robert McAlmon, *Being Geniuses Together*, reviewed by Kay Boyle (New York: Doubleday & Company, Inc., 1968), p. 9.

[26]So Eliot says in an interview with Donald Hall in *Paris Review Interviews*, 2d Series, ed. Van Wyck Brooks (New York: The Viking Press, 1963), p. 99.

[27]*After Strange Gods: A Primer of Modern Heresy* (London: Faber & Faber, 1934), p. 16 and Spender, "Remembering Eliot," in Tate, ed., *The Sewanee Review*, 74 (January-March 1966), 76.

[28]"The Hawthorne Aspect," *The Little Review*, 5 (August 1918), 49.

[29]From a letter to his brother, Henry Ware Eliot, Jr., dated September 8, 1914 in the Henry Ware Eliot Collection at the Houghton Library, Harvard.

[30]*The Autobiography of Bertrand Russell, 1914-44* (Boston, Mass.: Little, Brown & Company, 1956), p. 9.

[31]"Remembering Eliot," in Tate, ed., *The Sewanee Review*, 74 (January-March 1966), 69.

[32]"King Bolo & Others," in March & Tambimuttu, *T. S. Eliot*, p. 23.

[33]So he says in a letter to Isabella Stewart Gardner dated June-July 1915 in the Eliot Collection at the Houghton Library, Harvard.

[34] *Great Tom,* p. 43.

[35] "Eliot in Memory," *Yale Review,* 54 (June 1965), 638.

[36] The evidence is contained in a letter from T. S. Eliot to James Joyce dated January 4, 1931, in which Eliot commiserates with Joyce on the death of his father and remembers his feelings on the death of his own. This letter is among the Eliot-Joyce correspondence at the State University of New York at Buffalo.

[37] From a letter from Russell to Lady Ottoline Morrell dated July 1915, cited in *The Autobiography of Bertrand Russell, 1914-44,* p. 61.

[38] The evidence of Russell's numerous and generally candid letters to Lady Ottoline Morrell suggests the charge is untrue. Russell did everything he could to back out of going away with Eliot's wife. When he realized he could not do so without hurting Vivienne's feelings, he took her away reluctantly. Vivienne's only appeal for him was, he said, that of a child in pain. This conclusion is based on three undated, unpublished letters—one postmarked January 2, 1916—at the Humanities Research Center of the University of Texas at Austin.

[39] In a letter to Richard Aldington dated 6 November, 1921, Eliot says he suffers from "an aboulie and emotional derangement which has been a life-long affliction." At the same time he says there is nothing wrong with his mind. This letter is cited in Valerie Eliot's Facsimile Edition of *The Waste Land* (New York: Harcourt Brace Jovanovich, Inc., 1971), p. xxii. The original is at the Humanities Research Center of the University of Texas at Austin.

[40] Aldous Huxley remarked sex alone constituted the link between Tom and Vivienne Eliot, saying "one sees it in the way he looks at her—she's an incarnate provocation." Robert Gathorne-Hardy, *Ottoline at Garsington, 1915-18* (London: Faber & Faber, 1974), p. 207.

[41] *The Autobiography of Bertrand Russell, 1914-44,* pp. 9 and 69.

[42] *My Friends When Young: The Memoirs of Brigit Patmore,* ed. with introduction by Derek Patmore (London: William Heinemann Ltd., 1968), p. 90.

[43] In a letter from Eliot to Isabella Stewart Gardner of June-July 1915 in the Henry Ware Eliot Collection at Houghton Library, Harvard.

[44] "The First *Waste Land,*" in A. Walton Litz, ed., *Eliot in His Time: Essays on the Occasion of the Fiftieth Anniversary of The Waste Land* (Princeton: Princeton University Press, 1973), p. 57.

[45] See Donald Hall's interview with Eliot, *Paris Review Interviews,* p. 95 and Letter No. 50 from Ezra Pound to Harriet Monroe dated September 30, 1914, *Selected Letters of Ezra Pound, 1907-41,* ed. D. D. Paige (New York: New Directions, 1971), p. 40.

[46] Information contained in a letter to me from Valerie Eliot dated

September 23, 1975.

[47]Letter to Isabella Stewart Gardner of June-July 1915 in the Henry Ware Eliot Collection at the Houghton Library, Harvard.

[48]A letter from Eliot to his father dated March 1, 1917 and cited by Valerie Eliot in the Facsimile Edition of *The Waste Land,* p. xi is interesting in this regard.

[49]Robert Sencourt, *T. S. Eliot: A Memoir,* ed. Donald Adamson (New York: Dodd, Mead & Company, 1971), p. 63 and William Turner Levy & Victor Scherle, *Affectionately, T. S. E.: The Story of a Friendship, 1947-65* (Philadelphia & New York: J. B. Lippincott Company, 1968), p. 26.

[50]Sencourt, p. 163.

[51]*T. S. Eliot: Moments and Patterns* (Minneapolis: University of Minnesota Press, 1966), p. 9.

[52]*T. S. Eliot & Ezra Pound: Collaborators in Letters,* p. 7.

[53]Statement of editorial policy of *New Criterion,* 4 (January 1926), 2.

[54]This letter is dated July 12, 1922 and has been cited by various critics and biographers. The letter shows that Eliot feels himself beseiged by enemies in the London literary world who would be glad of his failure; it reveals an attitude much more characteristic of Pound than of Eliot. (The original is at the Humanities Research Center of the University of Texas at Austin.)

[55]Letters Nos. 195 & 293 to Kate Buss and T. S. Eliot, *Selected Letters,* ed. Paige, pp. 187 & 272.

[56]G. S. Fraser, cited by Matthews, *Great Tom,* pp. 53-54.

[57]"Remembering Eliot," in Tate, ed., *The Sewanee Review,* 74 (January-March 1966), 75-76.

[58]A letter to Aldington dated June 23, 1921 says, "These new yet old relationships involve immense tact and innumerable adjustments." This letter is at the Humanities Research Center of the University of Texas at Austin.

[59]Evidence of a letter from Eliot to John Quinn dated 5 November, 1919, and cited by Valerie Eliot in the Facsimile Edition of *The Waste Land,* p. xviii; by Donald Gallup, *T. S. Eliot & Ezra Pound: Collaborators,* p. 15, and by B. L. Reid, *The Man From New York: John Quinn and His Friends* (New York: Oxford University Press, 1968), p. 405.

[60]Valerie Eliot, ed., Facsimile Edition of *The Waste Land,* pp. xxiv-xxv.

[61]In a letter dated March 12, 1923 cited in B. L. Reid, *The Man From New York,* p. 582 and in Facsimile Edition of *The Waste Land,* p. xxvii.

[62]Robert Gathorne-Hardy, *Ottoline at Garsington, 1915-18,* pp. 101-

02.

[63] "T. S. E. - A Memoir," in Tate, ed., *The Sewanee Review*, 74 (January-March 1966), 35.

[64] Valerie Eliot states this emphatically in a letter to me dated September 23, 1975.

[65] Thus, he advised Wyndham Lewis not to settle in Paris and counseled John Gould Fletcher not to return to the United States. He told both men they would accomplish more by remaining in London. Eliot's letter to Lewis is dated 1921 and is at Cornell; the letter to Fletcher is dated August 14, 1928 and is at the Humanities Research Center of the University of Texas at Austin.

[66] See Eliot's Foreword to John Middleton Murry, *Katherine Mansfield & Other Literary Studies* (London: Constable & Company, 1959), p. ix.

[67] See Eliot's letter to Robert McAlmon dated May 2, 1921 cited in *Being Geniuses Together*, p. 9.

[68] This letter is headed "Sat. a.m.," in 1922 and was written without Eliot's knowledge from 9 Clarence Gate Gardens. It is at the Humanities Research Center of the University of Texas at Austin.

[69] According to Gallup, *T. S. Eliot & Ezra Pound: Collaborators*, p. 26.

[70] "The Expatriate as Fugitive," *Georgia Review*, 13 (Spring 1959), 8.

[71] From a letter to Lady Ottoline Morrell dated March 14, 1933 and written from Boston. The letter is at the Humanities Research Center of the University of Texas at Austin.

[72] *The Family Reunion*, Part I, sc. ii in T. S. Eliot, *The Complete Poems & Plays, 1909-1950* (New York: Harcourt Brace & World, Inc., 1952), p. 249.

[73] Evidence of letters to Allen Tate dated 26 March and 27 May, 1943 at Princeton University Library. Eliot's homesickness is attested in a letter to Lady Ottoline Morrell dated 9 February, 1933 at the Humanities Research Center of the University of Texas at Austin.

[74] Levy & Scherle, p. 119.

[75] For a picture of Eliot at this time, see Morley's reminiscence, "A Few Recollections of T. S. Eliot" in Tate, ed., *The Sewanee Review*, 74 (January-March 1966), 124-27.

[76] See Matthews, pp. 159-61.

[77] Valerie Eliot interviewed by Timothy Wilson, *The Observer*, February 20, 1972, p. 21. Matthews, p. 180.

[78] Levy & Scherle, pp. 128-29.

[79] Donald Hall interview, *Paris Review Interviews*, p. 109.

T. S. Eliot standing in the doorway of Faber & Gwyer,
March 1926
(reproduced by courtesy of the Houghton Library of Harvard University)

T. S. Eliot in May 1952
(photo taken by Harris Sobin and reproduced
courtesy of the Houghton Library, Harvard University)

JOYCE: THE ETERNAL RETURN

The Irish Tradition of Exile

Irish writers have traditionally been exiles from Ireland. Joyce is but one of a galaxy of exiles who became luminaries of English literature: Goldsmith, Sheridan, Wilde, Moore, and Beckett are others. Ireland's alienation of her artists is well known. Daniel Corkery, in *Synge and Anglo-Irish Literature,* remarks that almost all Irish writers who wrote in English have been expatriates for life.[1] Though Ireland has been so fertile a breeding ground for artists, she has not known until recently how to cultivate them. Poverty, nationalism, provincialism, not to say parochialism, Irish Catholicism, and censorship have all militated against that freedom of spirit and expression on which art thrives. Joyce's reasons for leaving Ireland were many, complex, and compelling. Some of them he shared with other exiles. Statements by George Bernard Shaw and George Moore in this regard are illuminating. Shaw declared, "My business in life could not be transacted in Dublin. . . . Every Irishman who felt that his business in life was on the higher planes of the cultural professions felt that he must have a metropolitan domicile and an international culture: that is, he felt that his first business was to get out of Ireland."[2] For Shaw in 1876, Dublin and the entire culture of Ireland were too provincial. So they were for Joyce a generation later. In the springtime of the Irish Literary Renaissance, Joyce's stance was obdurately European and international, anti-provincial and anti-Gaelic. There can be nothing more alienating than living in a country governed by another, speaking a language not one's own, yet Joyce could not approve the solution proposed by the Celtic revival. He believed literature in Gaelic was doomed to a sickly life and an early death. In "The Day of the Rabblement," he castigates the Irish as "the most belated race in Europe," and bids them follow European models, for he realizes that modern art will have to be international. Further, Joyce asserts there are no native models worth following.[3]   Joyce portrays Dublin in *Dubliners* and *A Portrait of the Artist as a Young Man* as intensely provincial, squalid, sordid, and paralysed, and Irish Catholicism as "the scullerymaid of Christendom."   The young Irish artist, as portrayed in Stephen Dedalus, frets at living on the fringes of European culture: "it wounded him to think that he would never be but a shy guest at the feast of the world's culture. . . ."[4]   In *Hail and Farewell*, George Moore affirms, "An Irishman must fly from Ireland if he would be himself."   Joyce agreed.   The fetters of nationalism, religion, and Dublin's mores constrained and stultified.   "I will not serve that in which I no longer believe, whether it call itself my home, my fatherland, or my church . . . I will try to express myself in some mode of life or art as freely as I can and as wholly as I can," declares Stephen.[5]   His integrity demands he leave Ireland and its sanctimonious pieties; so did Joyce's. George Moore goes on to observe that "art must be parochial in the beginning to become cosmopolitan in the end."[6]   Joyce agreed with this, too.   Like Eliot, he believed that a writer must be local and national before he can be international and universal.   "If I can get to the heart of Dublin I can get to the heart of all the cities of the world," he said.[7]   The paradox is explained when we consider that the writer must capture the little local world he knows best in order for the world to recognize the macrocosm in his microcosm.   But in Joyce's case it was essential that he leave Ireland in order to be able to write about her.

Joyce's Exile: Dispossession and Displacement

Among the personal reasons for Joyce's exile, there were stringent socioeconomic motives and spiritual ones no less exigent.   At an early age the writer suffered, as a result of his father, John Joyce's, decline in fortune, a sense of dispossession and displacement which threw him back on his own inner resources and bred an almost lunar sense of detachment. Art would enable him to create a world from which he could not be dispossessed.[8]   The eldest of ten surviving children, as a very young child James Joyce had known relative wealth and security in an upper middle class family.   When he was nine, the family's fortunes declined with the fall of Parnell, to whom they had been tied.   Parnell's downfall made an indelible impression on James

Joyce. James was called home after only two years at Clongowes Wood College, the foremost Jesuit college in Ireland, and became familiar with steadily deepening poverty. After this began that long series of stealthy removals to newer, poorer addresses which was to make Joyce acquainted with every corner of Dublin. It was a virtual *déclassement*. By the age of twelve Joyce had learned to look on his family's steady decline with a detachment that seemed like indifference. This decline was worsened by his father's fecklessness and could not be arrested by his mother's care and patience in trying to make ends meet. As the eldest and most brilliant child, James was favored above the others, and he and his brothers, after a spell with the Christian Brothers, received excellent free educations at Jesuit Belvedere College. Still, Stanislaus Joyce's *Diary* spells out in grim detail how poor the Joyces were by the time they reached their last home, 7 St. Peter's Terrace, Cabra, in fall 1902. Their father continued to drink up his meager pension and the children often had to subsist on one skimpy meal a day. Stanislaus called this last address "Bleak House," and describes how the brothers, after his mother died, had to safeguard their sisters from their father's drunken bully's rages.[9]   James, who loved his father for all his faults and even prided himself on having inherited his licentious temperament, made a joke even of hunger, calling himself Hunger personified.[10]   Nevertheless, he longed, like Stephen Dedalus, to leave behind the misrule and confusion of his father's house. A friend said that, after May Joyce's death in August 1903, there was no alternative for the Joyce children but flight.[11]   James Joyce's alternatives were to follow in his father's irresponsible footsteps; to make an attempt, like his brother Stanislaus, to help support the family, or to make a life for himself elsewhere. His temperament and artistic mission dictated the third course.

Quiet simply, there was no future for a young man of Joyce's antecedents, temperament, and talent in Dublin. Ulick O'Connor testifies that Dublin aborted the careers of many promising young men, and that there was a lack of opportunity at the turn of the century for men of Joyce's religion and class. "He was classic material for failure had he remained in Dublin. . . . Exile was the answer."[12]

Spiritual Exile

Joyce's spiritual alienation and exile from his homeland are much better documented than Pound's or Eliot's—most explicitly by the writer himself. Joyce's work is autobiographical and self-revelatory as the Americans' is not. Exile is one of Joyce's abiding obsessions. We should not simplemindedly confuse creator with creature, James Joyce with Stephen Dedalus, for Stephen is in part a mocking portrait of the artist as a young man. (He contains elements drawn from the characters of James *and* his brother Stanislaus and also from literary models of prototypical young aesthetes.)[13] Still, though Stephen Dedalus is a fictive, quasi-affectionate, quasi-ironic projection of Joyce himself, certain features and aspects of his case are Joyce's. We can safely conclude from Joyce's work that the author's soul, since its awakening, had been in exile. In *Portrait*, Stephen feels himself from the first an outsider, an observer, one who watches from the sidelines. He senses how different he is from others, how his feelings are not as theirs. "To merge his life in the common tide of other lives was harder for him than any fasting or prayer"; Stephen realizes himself incapable of loving others as he loves himself. He feels alien even to his own family.[14] He is isolated. Stephen's moments of greatest happiness and triumph occur alone. The artist creates alone and the creatures of his imagination are often company enough. To counteract his feeling of being on the edge of things, having an existence that is only marginal, Stephen has a habit of placing himself mentally at the center. Thus he is to himself center, but always on the world's circumference. Dedalus plays God.

Most of the incidents in Stephen's progressive alienation from family, nation, and church are drawn from Joyce's own life. At his first Christmas dinner with the grownups, young Stephen watches terrified a head-on conflict between the adherents of nationalism and religion. The immediate cause of the quarrel is the dead Parnell, who bade fair to be his country's redeemer but was condemned by the church. Young Stephen knows that country and church cannot both be right about Parnell; identifying himself with the fallen hero, he is ultimately to reject both nation and religion, for political disillusion is succeeded by religious disillusion. Later Stephen is forced to choose between God and the world, when the rector of Belvedere dangles before him the possibility of a priestly vocation. In this case, Stephen relinquishes neither the desire to be God nor his desire for the world; in choosing to be an artist he will be a surrogate god or priest of "eternal imagination, transmuting the daily bread of experience into the radiant body of everliving life."[15] His material will be profane experience, his mission semi-divine. The *Portrait,* with its dialectical structure, beautifully demonstrates how Stephen Dedalus' sexual, aesthetic, and religious impulses are fused or synthesized in art.[16]

Joyce's loss of faith was yet another form of alienation and spiritual exile. Religion was, for Joyce as for Stephen, the most difficult to reject of his early influences. His brother testifies James Joyce was, at an early age, "God-intoxicated," and that his work bears the hallmark of this intoxication he never completely threw off.[17] Just as Stephen's *non serviam* is not *non credo,* neither was Joyce wholly an infidel. Joyce's attitude to religion is very complex. Though he ceased to be a believing, practicing Catholic, his religion retained for him powerful symbolic and aesthetic values. He attended certain masses regularly, regarding the mass as a drama full of human significance, its sacred symbols invested with spiritual meaning. Joyce declared himself a man incapable of any belief, by which he perhaps meant that the artist must be capable of entertaining so many provisional beliefs, must be so protean in his capacity for belief, that he can be held to no single belief.[18] If it seems more accurate to say Joyce ceased to believe in God than that he continued to do so, one remembers that at the end of *A Portrait of the Artist,* Stephen tells Cranly he neither believes nor disbelieves in transsubstantiation and incarnation. He says, moreover, that he does not wish to conquer his doubt. For Joyce the universe is founded on incertitude and the void. It is worth remarking that neither Eliot nor Pound experienced any soul-shaking break with an all-embracing faith—indeed, Eliot in his exile found a faith to cling to.

Joyce's life and personality, as much as his vocation, dictated his removal from Dublin. As rebels generally do, he defined himself through rejection of existing institutions and conventions. A letter to Nora reviews his early life, citing all the objects of his disaffection in emphatic terms.

> My mind rejects the whole present social order and Christianity—home, the recognised virtues, classes of life, and religious doctrines. How could I like the idea of home? My home was simply a middle-class affair ruined

by spendthrift habits which I have inherited. My mother was slowly killed, I think, by my father's ill-treatment, by years of trouble, and by my cynical frankness of conduct. When I looked on her face as she lay in her coffin— a face grey and wasted with cancer—I understood that I was looking on the face of a victim and I cursed the system that made her a victim. We were seventeen in family [several children died in childbirth or infancy]. My brothers and sisters are nothing to me. One brother alone is capable of understanding me.

Six years ago I left the Catholic Church, hating it most fervently. I found it impossible for me to remain in it on account of the impulses of my nature. [Joyce began visiting whores in Nighttown at the age of fourteen.] I made secret war upon it when I was a student and declined to accept the positions it offered me. By doing this I made myself a beggar but I retained my pride. Now I make open war upon it by what I write and say and do. I cannot enter the social order except as a vagabond.[19]

This letter attests graphically Joyce's dislike of his native environment and shows how he felt himself to be a displaced person.

Joyce used his art as a weapon against the existing social order and against his acquaintances, who found themselves depicted in his work with scarcely human detachment and often with distaste. Richard Ellmann has described the reciprocity of life and art in Joyce's case; he plotted his life as fiction, in the process precipitating events he had imagined.

The fact that he was turning his life to fiction at the same time as he was living it encouraged him to feel a certain detachment from what happened to him, for he knew he could reconsider and re-order it for the purposes of his book. At the same time, since he felt dependent for material upon actual events, he had an interest in bringing simmering pots to a strong boil, in making the events through which he lived take on as extreme a form as possible. The sense that they were characters in his drama annoyed some of his friends . . . who did not much care for the role of culprit in a court where Joyce was both judge and prosecuting attorney. Joyce did not keep his book [*Stephen Hero*] to himself; he showed the manu-

> script to chosen friends, and . . . threatened some of them
> with the punishments he would mete out for slights suf-
> fered at their hands. . . . His art became a weapon which
> had an immediate effect upon his circle of acquaintances,
> and so altered the life it depicted.[20]

Thus, Joyce's life in Dublin provided the material for his art, but his shaping of that material into fiction altered life itself. One could say that Joyce *wrote* himself out of Ireland.

Joyce needed to feel persecuted and rejected. He used his exile, as Ellmann observes, as a reproach to others as well as a vindication of himself.[21] Joyce forged himself through resistance to the world. Writing was an act of rebellion by which he flung defiance at that world. Needing to leave Ireland in order to write about her, Joyce also needed to feel he had been driven out. From the first he identified himself with those who tried to save Ireland only to be betrayed by the old sow who eats her own farrow. Like many artists, Joyce mythologized his own personality; his life's models were scapegoats, victims, martyrs, and exiles. Pre-eminent among them were Christ, Parnell, and Ibsen. Christ was divinity which had taken on mortality only to be killed by men. Parnell had been betrayed by the very people he sought to liberate. Joyce identified strongly with Ibsen. Both writers came from similar family and social backgrounds. Both were estranged from the national and literary movements in their homelands; both became exiles. Stanislaus says his brother's discovery of Ibsen put an end to the religious mania James underwent at the age of sixteen as a result of his first fall from grace. Joyce admired in Ibsen his modernity, his eschewal of heroics, and his concentration on the commonplace, all of which he was to emulate.[22] As exile, Joyce felt an abiding interest in and affinity with Jews, those persecuted wanderers and outcasts. In contrast to Pound and Eliot, Joyce was not anti-Semitic—quite the contrary.

One finds in his work indications that Joyce engineered his own exile, and his letters contain admissions that he did so. In February 1905 he wrote his brother from Trieste that he had come to accept his present situation as "a voluntary exile," and added this would help him by supplying the necessary note with which to close his novel *Stephen Hero*.[23] It is on the note of exile that Stephen goes forth at the end of *A Portrait* "to en-counter for the millionth time the reality of experience and to forge in the smithy of my soul the uncreated conscience of my race."[24]   Joyce also declared that his rebellion and exile were engaged in, not only as protest against convention, but "with the intention of living in conformity with my moral nature."[25] For Joyce, then, exile was both positive and negative, a quest for his true self as well as a flight from the social snares he feared would entrap his soul.[26]

Writing as Exile—and Return

Exile was an essential condition of Joyce's art. He needed distance in space as well as time in order to write about Dublin and to create the uncreated conscience of his race. Dublin is Joyce's sole subject; the influence upon him of his native environment was so strong it was to absorb him for the rest of his life. There can be no better demonstration than Joyce's work of the truth of Eliot's dictum that the artist's subject matter is the first twenty-one years of his experience. Ireland's influence on Joyce was more powerful and profound than America's, via their respective home environments, on Pound or Eliot. Joyce's intensely autobiographical art, with its characteristically Irish satiric vein, necessitated his removal from Ireland. He encountered censorship with his earliest essays on "Drama and Life" and "The Day of the Rabblement."   His habit of putting family, personal friends and enemies, and recognizable events and places into his work, thinly disguised if at all, caused endless publishing difficulties even after Joyce quitted Ireland. His difficulties in publishing *Dubliners, A Portrait of the Artist,* and *Ulysses* have become legendary in the annals of avant garde literature's struggle for recognition.

Joyce's fiction is rooted in reality. His transcendent respect for reality is shown in his remark to Grant Richards: "he is a very bold man who dares to alter in the presentment, still more to deform, whatever he has seen and heard."[27] Joyce's naturalism is founded on his respect for facts and scrupulous fidelity to detail. His essay "Drama and Life" makes clear the author's belief that reality is a given and that the artist's task is to record and select experience in such a way as to bring out its latent significance. The artist should never lie or distort experience or indulge in false heroics. Joyce, like Stephen Dedalus, regretted the disparity between life as it is lived and life as it is usually portrayed in literature. Joyce's extraordinary fusion of symbolism and naturalism is achieved through selection of details that are rendered significant by incremental repetition in an ever expanding context. Meaning is conferred without falsification. Joyce said he had no imagination. Little in his work is wholly invented. Imagination shows itself most strikingly as an aspect of style and treatment rather than of subject matter, which was given him by life.

As Ellmann observes, writing is itself a form of exile.[28] It implies withdrawal and isolation. In order to write about anything well, one generally needs to be removed from one's subject in time or space. The assimilation and mastery of experience require detachment, and distance facilitates this. Joyce said that as long as he could write he could live anywhere,[29] but he could not write in Dublin. Exile was, as Anthony Burgess says, "the only means of objectifying an obsessive subject-matter."[30] His brother observed that writing normalized Joyce's mind; he wrote to free himself of obsessions. He wrote, says Stanislaus, "to make things clear to himself."[31] If writing was itself a form of exile, it was also a means of repatriation, of returning home and dwelling there in spirit, though not in body.[32] So Dedalus, having escaped the labyrinth he made, continues to hover over it in memory.

The Ambiguity of Joyce's Exile

Joyce's exile is full of ambiguities. Asked by a friend when he would return to Dublin, Joyce replied, "Have I ever left it?"[33] "The shortest way to Tara is via Holyhead."[34] The writer had to leave Dublin in order to dwell there in spirit for the rest of his life. All his life Joyce felt an intense ambivalence toward his homeland. He deliberately kept this love-hate relationship with Dublin on the boil. As time went by, his feelings for his birthplace mellowed somewhat, though they kept fluctuating. In 1906, only two years after his exile began, he was to say he had never felt at ease in any other city but Dublin, except Paris.[35] Yet, like Eliot and Pound, he had never been at home at home. From the distance of Rome, Joyce could perceive certain positive characteristics of Dublin that had been eclipsed by local squalor while he lived there. He pays tribute in "The Dead" to Dublin's ingenuous hospitality, conviviality, and natural beauty. Joyce found Dublin's small size an advantage, for it enabled him to view the city as a whole. As an artist whose hearing was as acute as his vision was dim, he always reveled in the "oral" quality of Dublin life, the feisty, gamy talk of her pubs, of which John Joyce was a master.

The restlessness and rootlessness of Joyce's European wanderings were counterbalanced by the fidelity and rootedness of his imagination. Because his mind was always fixed on Dublin, Joyce gives the impression of having been more rooted than Pound, who lacked such a lodestone. Both men, however, were restless and shared the tourist mentality. Richard Ellmann says:

> Joyce was a traveler by nature as well as necessity. When he had sufficiently complicated his life in one place, he preferred, instead of unraveling it, to move on to another. . . . One of the several reasons for his high spirits on leaving Dublin was that he had been forced into doing what he liked.[36]

Hélène Cixous points out that Joyce's "lack of stability and his refusal to adapt or settle down, which caused him to be constantly on the move . . . show that his departure was not an emigration towards a better . . . material life but a spiritual exile. . . ."[37] Even in Paris during the twenties, when Joyce was an "established" writer, he kept moving from one apartment to another as though reluctant to settle there permanently. Joyce's work is full of wanderlust. The image of the open road, land road or sea road, haunts Stephen from beginning to end of *A Portrait*. He is enchanted by the spell of "the white arms of roads, their promise of close embraces and the black arms of tall ships . . . their tale of distant nations," bidding him come.[38] In *Ulysses* Stephen spends the day dreaming of escape from Ireland, and Bloom (with a *Drang nach Suden* reminiscent of Joyce and his brother Stanislaus) dreams of the Promised Land. Yet, as Hélène Cixous observes, there really was no promised land for Joyce; "the only place both dear and necessary to him is the 'space' of the book and the only time that of the work in progress."[39] Joyce's life was absorbed by his writing more wholly than Pound's or Eliot's. This helps explain why the successive environments of his exile seem to have exerted a minimal influence on Joyce and to have made hardly any impression on his work. Since Joyce's obsessive themes were Dublin and himself, the world of his subsequent travels is reflected hardly at all— less than Eliot's surroundings are reflected in his, and considerably less than Pound's. If Joyce was a tourist, he was a preoccupied, purblind one. The only influence such cosmopolitan polyglot cities as Trieste, Zurich, and Paris seem to have had on Joyce's work is an influence on style.

That Joyce's subject is his own past distinguishes his work from Eliot's and Pound's, although his manner of universalizing it through myth insures as broad a scope. It is true that Joyce treats personal material impersonally, but Pound's work is more impersonal and Eliot's only obliquely personal. It can be said that Pound's and Eliot's past lay all before them, the attraction of Europe for both American writers being the immense treasure-house of an impersonal past. Both searched this with the aim of resurrecting forgotten glories and renewing them before men's sight. Joyce's personal past was behind him, though he was forever returning to rejuvenate it. In enabling him to do this, Europe played an important but catalytic, not substantive, role. Eliot found a personal stake in Europe's past, deliberately putting down roots where his ancestors had torn up theirs. Eliot and Joyce therefore afford an interesting contrast, for while Eliot's past is his future, Joyce's future is his past.

Joyce in Europe

In December 1902 Joyce left Dublin for Paris, ostensibly to continue at the Sorbonne the desultory medical studies he had begun in Ireland, but in fact to read, write—and starve. Why did Joyce choose Paris as the place of his first exile? Paris was the antithesis of Dublin and a much more dramatic leap away from home than London. Joyce had already visited London with his father. He never liked London, but cherished Paris as the "last of the human cities," maintaining its intimacy despite its size. In addition, he admired Paris as the center of rational civilization, while London was merely the center of material civilization.[40] Besides, too many Irish writers in exile had gone to London. Though he had looked forward to Paris as offering everything Dublin did not, after only two weeks there Joyce was homesick; he wrote his mother he would not want to live in Paris but to divide his existence between Paris and Dublin.[41] He went home to Dublin for Christmas and stayed a month.

In January 1903 Joyce returned to Paris and had a very thin time, supporting himself by writing reviews, giving English lessons, and borrowing. He was recalled home on Good Friday by a telegram from his father informing him his mother was dying. Thus Joyce's first Parisian exile lasted only six months; his brother called his first sojourn abroad a failure.[42] Joyce had accomplished little beyond the writing of a few reviews and poems, and a study of Aristotle that was to furnish the aesthetic theory presented in the final chapter of *A Portrait.* Much of his time in Paris he had spent starving, sponging on acquaintances, and writing cadging letters home.

A divided existence may radically alter one's perspective. No doubt Dublin looked smaller and drabber after six months in Paris. Joyce could view the city more objectively than before. It was the city to which he returned, Dublin of 1903-04, that he was to immortalize in *Ulysses.* In August 1903 May Joyce died of cancer of the liver. It would be a year and a half before her son set out on his travels once more. By the time he left Dublin for a more permanent exile, Joyce had written several essays, his epiphanies, the wan, *fin-de-siècle* poems of *Chamber Music,* three of the *Dubliners* stories, and ten chapters of *Stephen Hero,* his first novel and the dry-run for *A Portrait of the Artist as a Young Man.* For the most part, Joyce spent the eighteen months between April 1903 and October 1904 garnering the experience he was to make Stephen Dedalus' in the final chapter of *A Portrait* and the first three of *Ulysses.*

In June 1904 Joyce met Nora Barnacle, the event commemorated by Bloomsday. Nora became his companion in exile through all the vicissitudes of a turbulent career, but one of the social institutions against which Joyce rebelled was marriage. (He would not marry Nora for twenty-seven years—and then chiefly to secure the property rights of their children.) That one could not live in sin in Dublin in 1904 was another compelling reason for Joyce's departure with Nora for Europe. Furthermore, the difference in class and education made this liaison appear highly unsuitable, an affront to Joyce's family and a source of conflict with his friends in Dublin. The object of Joyce's love conspired with much else to make exile imperative. Although Joyce had to leave Ireland, it was important to him that a part of

Ireland accompany him physically into exile. Nora was that part. Joyce's Trieste Notebook says of Nora, "Wherever thou art shall be Erin to me."[43] Nora symbolized Ireland to Joyce.

In October 1904, assured of Nora's willingness to accompany him, Joyce determined on exile once more. As he had two years previously, he showed a certain insouciance in embarking on this important phase of his life. A week before their departure, the couple still did not know their destination. Joyce had applied for a Berlitz post anywhere in Europe. He was sorry when he thought he had secured one in London.[44] But that possibility fell through and his only instructions from Berlitz were to proceed to Switzerland. Joyce really wished to go to Paris, where he already felt at home, but he was ready for anything in Europe.

This was fortunate, for he was shunted from Zurich, where a position was supposed to await him but did not, to Trieste, where the situation was the same, to Pola, the naval base of the Austro-Hungarian Empire, a hundred and fifty miles south of Trieste. In this "back-of-God-speed place, a naval Siberia," as Joyce called it, he and Nora spent the first six months of their exile.[45] Pola was certainly the antipole of Paris, and must have made Nora, for whom being uprooted was not easy, homesick for Dublin. Joyce disliked the city and was ashamed of living there. It was a relief to be transferred in March 1905 to the Berlitz School in Trieste.

The Joyces spent ten years in Trieste. The decade 1905-15 was one of the most fertile of Joyce's career. During this period he completed the *Dubliners* stories, reconceived and rewrote *Stephen Hero* as *A Portrait of the Artist,* wrote his play, *Exiles,* and brought *Ulysses* as far as the three books of the Telemachiad. To achieve the necessary perspective and focus to present Dublin and his relations with that city in all their *quidditas* and *claritas,* Joyce needed the distance given by exile in Trieste and the lapse of ten years during which he reshaped *Stephen Hero* into *A Portrait.* Joyce recognized with satisfaction that he had made great strides as a writer since leaving Dublin for Trieste.[46]

In addition to literary progeny, the Joyces' two children, Giorgio and Lucia, were born in Trieste. For all his contempt for marriage and bourgeois conventions, friends and biographers of Joyce agree he was a family man, even a paterfamilias, though his children were born out of wedlock and he regarded paternity as a legal fiction. Joyce imported more of his family and Ireland to

Trieste in the persons of his brother Stanislaus and his sisters Eileen and Eva. Abroad Joyce learned to be the Dubliner he could not be at home. In later years in Europe, he always extended a warm welcome to visitors from Dublin. The Joyces' apartments were liberally decorated with souvenirs of Ireland, including a carpet with a design of the River Liffey and a cork-framed picture of Cork. Their home furnishings progressed from threadbare to solidly bourgeois.

Though Trieste grew on Joyce, his feelings about the city were ambivalent, as his feelings about Dublin had been. Indeed, he saw parallels between Trieste and Dublin in their size, irredentist temper, and the fact that the citizens of both spoke a language foreign to them. The language of the Joyce household became and remained Italian, with a flavoring of Triestine dialect. Joyce liked the Latinate culture of Trieste, which for him outweighed the Slav and Teutonic strains. He liked Trieste's ramshackle air. In retrospect he remembered how kind people had been to him there, although he also records how cruel the Triestine women were to unmarried, pregnant Nora.[47]

At the same time as Joyce recognized his status as that of "voluntary exile," he chafed against it and wished to return to Dublin. A letter to Stanislaus, written shortly before his son was born in July 1905, shows that Joyce did not yet regard his exile as permanent, that he had embraced it as a means of demonstrating to the people back home that he could make good elsewhere. "The very degrading and unsatisfactory nature of my exile angers me and I do not see why I should continue to drag it out with a view to returning 'some day' with money in my pocket and convincing the men of letters that, after all, I was a person of talent." Instead, James proposes to Stanislaus that they both save up to buy a cottage in the suburbs of Dublin where the three of them and the baby might live.[48] This scheme was abandoned; instead, Stanislaus was persuaded to join the Joyces in Trieste a year after their own arrival in the Austro-Hungarian Empire. Stanislaus was of inestimable help in holding the Joyce household together. He was, as he describes in his book of that title, his brother's keeper, rescuing him from financial scrapes and bouts of dissipation. It was in Trieste that Joyce suffered his first eye trouble. (Weak eyes and nearsightedness ran in the Joyce family.) Joyce's poor vision is an important factor in explaining why the sights of Europe have left so little impress on his work. Quite simply, though Joyce was a boulevarider and a frequenter of cafés, restaurants, and bars, he had little time and less vision for sightseeing. Thus, from Rome in 1906, he absurdly claims that Dublin is "more beautiful naturally in my opinion than what I have seen of England, Switzerland, France, Austria, or Italy."[49] But what, one asks, had Joyce *seen* of these countries? One suspects that memory no less than near-sightedness—Dublin being the irremovable scrim through which he viewed all other places—blurred his vision.

In 1906 Joyce went to Rome as a bank clerk, spending nine months there. He detested Rome, mostly because of the conditions under which he lived there. He had never undergone such drudgery as he did at the bank translating commercial correspondence nine hours a day and giving English lessons when he returned home at night, exhausted. Though he had valuable ideas for writing—the germ of *Ulysses* was planted in Rome and the city helped inspire the finest of Joyce's short stories, "The Dead"—Joyce complained he had neither time nor energy to put pen to paper in Rome. That it was the center of Catholicism was probably another reason for Joyce's dislike for the Eternal City; he found it as venal, corrupt, and moribund as Dublin. Before returning to Trieste, he wrote his brother he himself felt half dead.

> I have come to the conclusion that it is about time I made up my mind whether I am to become a writer or a patient Cousins. I foresee that I shall have to do other work as well but to continue as I am at present would certainly mean my mental extinction. It is months since I have written a line and even reading tires me.... I have gradually slid down until I have ceased to take any interest in any subject. I look at God and his theatre through the eyes of my fellow-clerks so that nothing surprises, moves, excites, or disgusts me.[50]

Exile's Return

While living in Trieste, Joyce made three trips back to Dublin. Ill luck attended each of these, and the last was so traumatic that Joyce decided never to return to Ireland again. Thereafter his exile became permanent. In the summer of 1909, Joyce took his son to Dublin, leaving his wife and daughter in Trieste. His chief purpose in making this trip was to get *Dubliners* published. A contract had been signed for the book by the English publisher, Grant Richards, in February 1906. Richards, however, had reneged on this contract at the end of the year. He foresaw publishing difficulties because the printer found some of the language in the stories obscene. Joyce made concessions and protested in vain. He subsequently submitted his manuscript to the Dublin publisher, Maunsel, and in August 1909 succeeded in negotiating a second contract for the book. Maunsel, however, were to raise similar objections to those Richards had; in addition, they objected to Joyce's habit of using actual names of places and people as libelous. In Dublin Joyce also looked into the possibility of an Italian lectureship at the National University, but decided against it. His trip home was ruined by the treachery of one of his friends, Cosgrave (Lynch in *A Portrait*). Cosgrave told Joyce that when he had been courting Nora in 1904, she had been "two-timing" him with Cosgrave. Joyce's suspicious nature and inherent persecution complex made it impossible for him to disbelieve this, despite Nora's fidelity and innocence. He wrote her in accusation, even demanding to know whether Giorgio were his son. Joyce remained shattered until the lie was exposed by his friend Byrne (Cranly in *A Portrait*) and by Stanislaus, to whom Cosgrave had once confided his interest in Nora but total lack of success with her. Restored to confidence, Joyce humbly asked Nora's forgiveness. Out of the wound opened in his soul by this supposititious cuckoldry he wrote his only play, *Exiles*. Richard Rowan, the protagonist, is a distinguished writer who returns to Dublin from exile. There he brings about a love affair between his wife, Bertha, and a friend of his and childhood sweetheart of hers, Robert Hand. Whether Robert actually makes love to Bertha remains doubtful. The important thing is that Rowan believes his best friend has possessed his wife and that, in wittingly and willingly bringing this about, he possesses them both. At the end, Robert goes abroad while Richard and Bertha, still exiles, remain in Dublin.

On returning there, Joyce declared he felt a stranger in Dublin and loathed Ireland and the Irish.[51] Nevertheless, a month after returning to Trieste, Joyce was back in Dublin once more, this time with the object of starting Dublin's first cinema. He was joined in this, the Volta project, by four Trieste businessmen. The scheme was a failure; the Volta opened in December

1909, only to close down six months later. Nor was Joyce's project of becoming an agent in Trieste for Irish tweeds any more successful. Meanwhile, in Trieste, Nora and Stanislaus were desperately trying to cope with dunning creditors and a threatening landlord. Joyce sought to distract and excite his wife with eager anticipations of their reunion in love letters so scatologically obscene they have been withheld from publication.[52]

Joyce had not intended to make his final trip to Ireland. In the summer of 1912 he acceded to Nora's desire to see her home and family again. Nora, accompanied only by Lucia, left for Dublin. Joyce found he could not endure being without her and followed with Giorgio. In his determination to make Maunsel publish *Dubliners* after three years of nitpicking complaints about this and that detail as sure to offend Irish and English sensibilities, Joyce had good reason for returning to Dublin. The outcome was disastrous. Although he made every effort to comply with his publishers in removing each offensive item from his stories, and even agreed to pay sixty per cent of the cost of printing, Maunsel destroyed both the type and sheets of Joyce's book. The author contrived to rescue only a single copy. The vexed story of *Dubliners'* publication, and of how Grant Richards, the original publisher, finally brought it out in 1914, was told by Joyce in a letter to the Irish press, reprinted by Ezra Pound in *The Egoist.*[53] Joyce now had just cause to consider himself persecuted by his own people. He resolved never to set foot in Ireland again and he never did.[54] His experience in Dublin in 1912 set the seal on his exile, now to be lifelong.

Zurich

World War I flushed the Joyces out of Trieste. They were compelled to leave when the Italian military authorities ordered the city's partial evacuation in spring 1915. Influential students of Joyce's secured an exit permit for the Joyce family, who made their way to neutral Switzerland. (Stanislaus, an outspoken irrendentist, was not so fortunate; he was interned for the duration of the war.) Joyce now settled in Zurich. Everything except the cold, damp climate suited him. The city was *bürgerlich* but international. During the war, Zurich was filled with distinguished refugees, many of them artists. It became a center for avant garde experimentation in the arts, and provided a favorable climate for the gestation of *Ulysses,* the greater part of which Joyce wrote in Zurich. Joyce continued to give English lessons privately. He finally achieved a measure of prosperity, largely through the tireless efforts on his behalf of Ezra Pound and the generous bequests, continued for life, of Harriet Shaw Weaver. *A Portrait of the Artist* was serialized in Miss Weaver's *The Egoist* from February 1914 to September 1915, and Pound then arranged for the serialization of *Ulysses* in the *Little Review.*[55]

After the war Joyce returned to Trieste but discovered it much changed. Postwar prices were high and the atmosphere of the city distinctly grimmer. Joyce was ready to move again but did not know where. In Trieste the writer now shared an apartment with his brother, sister, brother-in-law, his own wife, and four children. It was difficult to write under such crowded conditions and Joyce even considered a holiday in London and Ireland to help him finish the Circe episode of *Ulysses.* In the summer of 1920 Ezra Pound, also at loose ends at this stage of his career, was staying at Sirmione, one of his favorite haunts on Lake Garda. Though Pound had helped Joyce publish *A Portrait* and *Dubliners* and *Ulysses* in serial form and had procured for him both money and publicity, the two writers had never met. The meeting which took place on June 8, 1920 was important, for Pound persuaded Joyce to make Paris his next home.

Paris

So Joyce returned to Paris, the starting point of his exile, in July 1920. He came intending a short visit but remained for twenty years. Thanks to Pound's advance publicity, Joyce was a celebrity in the Paris literary world during his second stay there. One of the attractions for him of Paris was the high esteem in which authors are held in France.[56] Paris was *the* place to be in the twenties, a haven for artists from all over the world, many of whom, like Joyce, were exiles.

In Paris Joyce formed the center of one of many artistic circles. Though he never overcame his distaste for literary movements and journalists and sometimes held himself aloof, Joyce's Parisian sojourn was sociable and he enjoyed a *gloire du cénacle.* From the first, acquaintances were extraordinarily obliging and helpful in assisting Joyce with domestic as well as literary problems. Apartments, furniture, and household utensils were lent him freely, and, as his eyesight deteriorated, friends also gave him secretarial help. Sylvia Beach in particular, as her correspondence with Joyce shows, turned herself into an ever-willing amanuensis.[57] Paris was good to Joyce. Though he thought of moving to England in the thirties to establish residence there so his children might inherit his property under English law, and though he and Nora spent several holidays there, they never liked England enough to stay long.

In Paris Joyce finished *Ulysses,* revising the Nighttown episode nine times and writing the three books of the Nostos. *Ulysses* was completed, after seven years' work, on October 30, 1921, Pound's birthday, from which he dated the end of the Christian and the beginning of a new pagan age, the Pound Era. Joyce despaired of finding a publisher for *Ulysses* after the suppression of several episodes in serial form and the refusal of several publishers to undertake so daring and experimental a book. Sylvia Beach's Shakespeare and Company came to Joyce's rescue, publishing an edition of one thousand copies and paying Joyce a very handsome royalty. *Ulysses* appeared on Joyce's fortieth birthday. When the French edition, most of which had been subscribed in advance, was sold out, The Egoist Press of London imported French sheets for a private English edition of two thousand copies. Official American and English editions were not published until 1934 and 1936, respectively, after battles against piracy, confiscation, and the charge of obscenity in Anglo-Saxondom had been won.

A year after publishing *Ulysses,* Joyce began his herculean labors on *Finnegans Wake.* This last book took him seventeen years to write. He was severely handicapped by failing eyesight, undergoing a total of eleven eye operations and temporarily losing the sight of one eye. *Finnegans Wake* was published only a year before the outbreak of the Second World War.

As the First World War had driven Joyce from Trieste to Zurich, the second was to compel him to leave Paris. In 1939-40 the Joyces moved first to St. Gérand-le-Puy, then to nearby Vichy. In December 1940, Joyce returned to Zurich once more —this time to die. Years of hunger and heavy drinking had played havoc with Joyce's digestion; the perforated duodenal ulcer from which he died on January 13, 1941 was the result of a longstanding condition.

Exile was the subject of much of Joyce's work. Most of his major characters—Gabriel Conroy, Richard Rowan, Stephen Dedalus, Leopold Bloom, and H. C. Earwicker—are physical or spiritual exiles. Exile was also the means by which Joyce's work was accomplished. One concludes that the forces compelling Joyce to leave Ireland were stronger and more irresistible than those which impelled Pound and Eliot to leave America. Had they remained, Pound and Eliot might still have been writers, but given the fact that Joyce's sole subject was Dublin, a Dublin scathingly presented down to the last sordid detail, Joyce would never have been published had he remained there.

Of the five stages of Joyce's European hegira, as he called it—Pola-Trieste-Zurich-Paris-Zurich—one feels it did not much matter to him where he was, so long as he could look homeward without ruth and write. Although when he wrote, whatever he heard, saw, or felt became grist to his mill, the influence of his European surroundings on both writer and work appears minimal.[58] Joyce's devotion to his art, however, was so all-absorbed and all-absorbing that everywhere he went others got caught up in the vortex of his coldly passionate and ruthless obsession and were often sacrificed willy nilly to his needs. His mismanagement of everyday life through improvidence and irresponsibility were the obverse of his control over his art. Few writers have left behind letters so punctuated by demands, requests, and entreaties for money. Joyce might therefore be said to have exerted an influence on his human environment disproportionate to its influence on him. His most important and lasting influence, of course, has been on the world in which he lived his entire life— the patria of letters. There he knew no exile.

NOTES

[1] *Synge & Anglo-Irish Literature: A Study* (Cork: Cork University Press, 1947), p. 4.

[2] Preface to *Immaturity* (New York: William H. Wise & Company, 1930), p. xxxviii.

[3]"The Day of the Rabblement," *The Critical Writings of James Joyce*, eds. Ellsworth Mason and Richard Ellmann (New York: The Viking Press, 1959), p. 70.

[4]*A Portrait of the Artist as a Young Man*, Compass Books (New York: The Viking Press, 1956), p. 180. Hereafter referred to as *Portrait*.

[5]*Ibid.*, p. 247.

[6]*Ave, Hail & Farewell* (New York: D. Appleton & Company, 1925), I, 5.

[7]Richard Ellmann, *James Joyce* (New York: Oxford University Press, 1959), p. 520.

[8]As Hélène Cixous points out in *The Exile of James Joyce* (New York: David Lewis, 1972), p. 4.

[9]*The Dublin Diary of Stanislaus Joyce*, ed. George H. Healey (Ithaca: Cornell University Press, 1962), pp. 27 & 39. Hereafter referred to as *Diary*.

[10]Ellmann, p. 66.

[11]C. P. Curran, *James Joyce Remembered* (New York: Oxford University Press, 1968), p. 70.

[12]*The Joyce We Knew* (Cork: The Mercier Press, 1967), pp. 8-9.

[13]Stanislaus Joyce points out *A Portrait* is not an autobiography but an artistic creation in *My Brother's Keeper: James Joyce's Early Years* (New York: The Viking Press, 1958), p. 17. In his *Diary*, Stanislaus even calls it "a lying autobiography" (p. 25). To see how Joyce conflated his own with Stanislaus' character to produce Stephen's, it is necessary to read his brother's two books. The chief characteristics Stanislaus contributed to Dedalus are boredom, sullenness, premature age, and a loathing of Ireland more virulent than Joyce's. His brother reveals that James had a much sunnier and more sociable temerament than Stephen's and was more of an athlete, being a strong walker and good swimmer. Maurice Beebe is interesting on the subject of the distance between Joyce and Stephen and the number of literary models who contributed something to Joyce's portrait of the artist as a young man—Joyce himself emphasized Stephen's age. See Maurice Beebe, *Ivory Towers and Sacred Founts: The Artist as Hero in Fiction from Goethe to Joyce* (New York: New York University Press, 1964), pp. 264-67.

[14]See *Portrait*, pp. 98, 151, 166.

[15]*Ibid.*, p. 221.

[16]The process culminates in the two final chapters, though adumbrated in the first three. Probably the best discussion of the structure of the *Portrait* is Hugh Kenner's "The *Portrait* in Perspective" in his *Dublin's Joyce* (London: Chatto & Windus, 1955), pp. 109-33.

[17]*My Brother's Keeper*, p. 139.

[18] In a letter to Stanislaus dated May 1905, *Letters of James Joyce,* ed. Richard Ellmann (London: Faber & Faber, 1966), II, 89. Hereafter referred to as *Letters.*

[19] Letter dd. 29 August 1904, *Letters,* II, 48.

[20] Ellmann, p. 154. It is necessary to point out that Joyce turned life directly into fiction only while he was in Dublin; thereafter he was dependent on memory for his materials.

[21] Ellmann, p. 113.

[22] *My Brother's Keeper,* pp. 84, 87, & 95.

[23] *Letters,* II, 84. In a letter to Stanislaus in May 1905, Joyce says he used the false attitude toward him of his friends as "an excuse for escape" from Ireland, *Ibid.,* p. 89.

[24] *Portrait,* p. 253.

[25] Letter to Stanislaus dd. 19 July 1905, *Letters,* II, 99.

[26] Hélène Cixous, p. 453.

[27] Letter dd. 5 May 1906, *Letters,* II, 134.

[28] Ellmann, p. 114.

[29] *Ibid.*

[30] *Re Joyce* (New York: W. W. Norton & Company, 1965), p. 27.

[31] *My Brother's Keeper,* p. 34 and Ellmann, p. 275.

[32] Hélène Cixous, p. 484.

[33] Ellmann, p. 302; see also Curran, p. 100.

[34] *Portrait,* p. 251.

[35] Letter to Stanislaus dd. 25 September 1906, *Letters,* II, 166.

[36] Ellmann, p. 189.

[37] Hélène Cixous, p. 530.

[38] *Portrait,* p. 253.

[39] Hélène Cixous, p. 17.

[40] See Ellmann, p. 523 and Mary and Padraic Colum, *Our Friend James Joyce* (New York: Doubleday & Company, 1958), p. 232.

[41] Letter dd. December 15, 1902, *Letters,* II, 21.

[42] *My Brother's Keeper,* p. 197.

[43] Cited by Hélène Cixous, p. 515; the Trieste Notebook is reproduced in Robert Scholes & Richard M. Kain, eds., *The Workshop of Daedalus* (Evanston: Northwestern University Press, 1965).

[44] Letter to Nora Barnacle dd. September 29, 1904, *Letters,* II, 57.

[45] Letter to Mrs. Wm. Murray dd. New Year's Eve 1904, *Letters of James Joyce,* ed. Stuart Gilbert (New York: The Viking Press, 1957), I, 57.

[46] Letter to Stanislaus dd. July 12, 1905, *Letters,* II, 93.

[47] For Trieste seen in retrospect, see Herbert Gorman, *James Joyce* (New York: Rinehart & Company, 1939), p. 143 and cf. a letter to Stanislaus dd. July 12, 1905, *Letters,* II, 93.

[48]*Ibid., Letters,* II, 96-97.

[49]Letter to Stanislaus dd. September 25, 1906, *Letters,* II, 166.

[50]Letter dd. March 1, 1907, *Letters,* II, 217.

[51]Letter to Nora dd. October 27, 1909, *Letters,* II, 255.

[52]These letters, written in December 1909, are in the Cornell Joyce Collection.

[53]See "A Curious History" in *The Egoist,* 1 (15 January, 1914), 26-7. See also *Letters,* II, 291-92 & 324-25. A letter from Joyce to his literary agent, J. B. Pinker, in July 1917 recapitulates the publishing difficulties of *Dubliners* and adds those of *A Portrait*—see *Letters,* II, 399.

[54]The Colums say Joyce's exile began in earnest in 1912, *Our Friend James Joyce,* p. 102. C. P. Curran maintains Joyce thought of visiting Ireland in the twenties (letters confirm he thought of a visit in summer, 1920) and the thirties, but that he always pleaded his work as an excuse for not going. *James Joyce Remembered,* pp. 101-01.

[55]*Ulysses* was serialized in *The Little Review* from April 1918 to July-August 1920, ending with the Nausicaa episode, which was prosecuted for obscenity in February 1921. John Quinn defended *Ulysses* unsuccessfully.

[56]Stuart Gilbert, Introduction to *Letters,* I, 23.

[57]Joyce's correspondence with Sylvia Beach is in the Sylvia Beach Collection at the University of Buffalo.

[58]Stanislaus said his brother claimed he absorbed rather than saw things and that he missed very little in this process of absorption—*My Brother's Keeper,* p. 120.

Joyce in Dublin in 1904
(photo taken by C. P. Curran and reproduced by
courtesy of the Beinecke Library of Yale University)

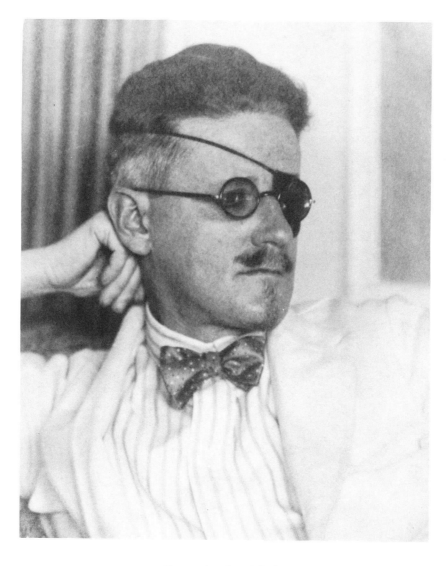

Joyce in the thirties
(photo by Bernice Abbot,
reproduced by courtesy of the Beinecke Library)

INDEX